P-51 MUSTANG

PART 1: NA-73X THROUGH P-51A -- THE ALLISON-ENGINED VARIANTS

in detail & scale

by Bert Kinzey
and Haagen Klaus
Art by Rock Roszak

TABLE OF CONTENTS

COPYRIGHT 2025 BY DETAIL & SCALE

CONTRIBUTORS AND SOURCES

Stan Piet   Dana Bell   Gerald Balzer   Scott Manning
Lloyd Jones   Paul Boyer   Stan Parker   Rick Troutman
Chip Michie   Andrey Kozlov   National Museum of the U. S. Air Force
Yanks Air Museum   Planes of Fame Museum

ISBN: 979-8-3071907-2-2

In 1996, Detail & Scale published two books on the P-51 Mustang, the first covering the variants up through the P-51C, and the second on the P-51D and subsequent versions. Now, almost three decades later, we are greatly expanding our coverage of the Mustang, which is one of the most iconic fighter aircraft ever produced. This time we are publishing three volumes on the P-51, and each is considerably larger than the books released in 1996. This first part takes a look at the Allison-engined versions of the Mustang in great detail. Part 2 will include the first of the Rolls Royce/Packard Merlin-engined variants, the P-51B and P-51C, along with their photo-recon versions. Finally, Part 3 will cover the P-51D and subsequent variants.

1996

2025

Front Cover Photo: The P-51-NA was the first American variant of the Mustang to go into production. It was also flown by the British as the Mustang Mk. IA. This version could be easily identified by its unique armament of four 20mm cannons mounted in the wings. (North American Aviation [NAA] via Piet)

Rear Cover Photo: Colors and details of the instrument panel in a P-51A are revealed in this photograph taken of the P-51A at the Yanks Air Museum. Additional photographs taken in the cockpit of this Mustang can be found in the Allison-Engined Mustang Details chapter. (Kinzey)

INTRODUCTION

A high front view illustrates the features of a P-51-NA as it flies along the coastline of southern California. This was the second of the Allison-engined Mustangs, following the British Mustang Mk. I, to go into production and the first to be flown operationally by the U. S. Army. Some were converted to armed photographic-reconnaissance aircraft and redesignated as F-6As, while others served with the British as Mustang Mk. IAs. (NAA via Piet)

This book is the first in a three volume series that covers the P-51 Mustang, one of the most iconic fighter aircraft ever designed. It begins with a history of the development and operational use of the Allison-engined variants. The Mustang initially came into being to help provide the British with as many first-line fighters as possible at a time when they were needed the most as Germany prepared to invade England. Lt. Benjamin Kelsey, the head of the Army Air Corps Pursuit Projects Office at Wright Field, Ohio, used his knowledge of aerodynamics and his ingenuity to ensure that the U. S. Army would also acquire the Mustang as America's entry into World War II became more imminent with each passing day. The history chapter not only covers the development of the early Mustang variants, it also summarizes their valuable contributions to the Allied war effort.

The next chapter takes a closer look at each of the Allison-engined variants, pointing out their differences and features with an informative text and in photographs. The A-36 dive bomber version gets special treatment with no less than thirty-six photographs, many of which illustrate its unique features. In the variants chapter, both the fighter and photo-recon variants of each version are covered. Scale drawings are provided for the production variants, and differences and unique features are indicated on these drawings.

Next comes the Allison-engined Mustang Details chapter that provides in-depth coverage of the common details of these variants. Nine different sections in this chapter include

more than 125 photographs that illustrate the details more extensively than any other publication. All but two of these are in color and were taken specifically for Detail & Scale.

As with all Detail & Scale Series publications, the book concludes with a Modelers Section that reviews the scale model kits of the Allison-engined Mustangs that have been issued to date. These objective reviews point out the good and not-so-good points about each kit and make recommendations as to which ones are best for scale modelers to use.

The extensive coverage presented in this book would not have been possible without the generous assistance of the contributors and sources listed on the previous page. A very special thanks is extended to the National Museum of the U. S. Air Force for allowing the author to photograph the A-36A at the museum in considerable detail and also to the Yanks Air Museum for allowing detail photography of their P-51A. Additionally, Scott Manning took detail photos of another P-51A at the Planes of Fame Museum.

Historical photographs were generously provided by Stan Piet, Gerald Balzer, and Dana Bell from their extensive collections. The Research Division at the National Museum of the U. S. Air Force also provided assistance as the authors conducted research there.

Contributions to the Modelers Section were made by Paul Boyer, Stan Parker, Rick Troutman, and Chip Michie. To all of the contributors, Detail & Scale expresses sincere appreciation for their assistance which made this publication possible.

ALLISON-ENGINED MUSTANG HISTORY

The origin of the North American P-51 Mustang was spurred by the German advance through Europe beginning in 1939. It is quite possible that the P-51 would never have come into existence if not for Great Britain's urgent need for as many fighter planes as they could obtain. Beginning with the prototype NA-73X, seen here in a later test flight in 1941, the P-51 Mustang became one of the most historically significant military aircraft of the twentieth century. (G. Balzer Collection)

The path that led to the development and production of the P-51 Mustang began with the first shot fired in Germany's invasion of Poland on September 1, 1939. Great Britain and Germany declared war upon each other days later, and very soon thereafter, Hitler and his field marshals shifted attention to Western Europe. In the United States, war seemed far away, but on the other side of the Atlantic Ocean apprehension grew daily. The success of the Nazi blitzkrieg across the low countries and France by June 1940 reinforced the perception that nothing could blunt the German onslaught. It appeared to be just a matter of time, perhaps only a few months, before England would be facing the Germans alone.

German war planners developed the first draft of a series of contingency plans for an invasion of England in 1939. Hitler continued to see a negotiated neutrality with the United Kingdom as the most advantageous strategy, at least in the short term. Still, invasion proposals continued to be refined. Their final scheme was overly ambitious, but it realistically called for what the Germans would have to do in to order mount a successful invasion. It involved a large-scale amphibious assault against Great Britain that required total German air and naval dominance to succeed. Nazi war planners increasingly saw such preconditions as improbable. In London, the British leadership knew they needed war materials and weapons in great quantities, and fast. Nothing was of higher priority than fighter planes to defend the island nation against Luftwaffe bombers. Hawker and Supermarine were manufacturing Hurricanes and Spitfires as fast as they could, but production rates could not meet the demand.

Origins and Development of the NA-73X

The joint Anglo-French Purchasing Commission traveled to the United States in January 1940 hoping to acquire additional Curtiss P-40s. They also expressed interest in the improved Curtiss P-46 which was then under development. Unfortunately, the Curtiss production lines were operating at maximum capacity. To solve this problem, the Commission approached James H. "Dutch" Kindelberger, the president of California-based North American Aviation (NAA), a company

that the British had an established relationship with. The RAF was actively acquiring their T-6 Texan trainer, but these were not the fighters so desperately needed. North American had the production line capacity, but they had never developed or manufactured a fighter. The Commission asked Kindelberger if North American could produce Curtiss fighters under license. Later during World War II, such arrangements become standard practice where one company manufactured another's design. This approach was not yet adopted in 1940, and North American was not at all interested in building another company's airplane. To the contrary, they had strong ambitions to develop their own fighter.

In response to the request to build P-40s under license, North American informed the British that it could create an even better fighter than the P-40 and be at least as capable as the P-46, while still using the same Allison V-1710 inline engine. Reports have been published stating that North American stipulated in the contract that this would be accomplished in only 120 days, but in fact there was no such guarantee. Nevertheless, North American did assure the British that the plane could be designed and produced quickly. The British required that the unit cost of each aircraft be no more than $40,000.

On April 10, 1940, the proposal was accepted by the Anglo-French Purchasing Commission. The prototype, assigned North American's model number NA-73, was ordered along with 320 production airframes on May 29, 1940. It was a risky act, equal parts reflecting faith in NAA and a desperate need for more RAF fighters. The following month, France fell to the Germans, and England was indeed alone. North American had obtained the formal release to sell the NA-73 to the British on May 4, 1940. As part of this legal formality, the head of the Army Air Corps Pursuit Projects Office at Wright Field, First Lieutenant Benjamin S. Kelsey, included the stipulation that two aircraft from the first production run be turned over to Wright Field for testing. Kelsey saw an opportunity; the U.K. would buy for the U. S. Army two promising aircraft which it did not then have the funds to purchase for itself.

If asked to name the American military personnel who made the most significant contributions to victory in World War

II, Dwight Eisenhower, George Patton, Douglas MacArthur, and Chester Nimitz come to mind. Lieutenant Kelsey would also need to be on that list. With a degree in aeronautical engineering from MIT, Lt. Kelsey was qualified in aircraft design and performance. He also ingeniously found the means and the money to keep certain programs going until America's entry into the war insured their funding and their success. Promotions were few and far between during the 1930s, and lieutenants often held positions of great responsibility such as Kelsey's post. He exhibited unique qualities of leadership, engineering acumen, and an ability to creatively work around highly rigid, restrictive, and conservative USAAC design regulations and anemic pre-war budgets. Lt. Kelsey's accomplishments included being the single-most important figure driving forward the development and production of the Allison V-1710 engine, the Bell P-39 Airacobra, and the Lockheed P-38 Lightning. Yet, Kelsey's most important contribution to World War II was arguably his move to acquire these two early British aircraft that would eventually evolve into the P-51 Mustang.

Raymond H. Rice was North American's Chief Engineer, Edgar Schmued was their Chief of Design, and Ed Horkey served as Chief Aerodynamicist. These men worked as a team day and night, seven days a week, to produce the new fighter design as quickly as possible. In a few weeks, their team had grown to more than forty engineers. Further, Lt. Kelsey's background as an aeronautical engineer allowed him to understand the importance of recent studies on laminar flow airfoils by the National Advisory Committee on Aeronautics (or NACA, the forerunner to NASA). Kelsey saw this feature as advantageous for the new fighter, and NACA's Eastman Jacobs was assigned to the North American team.

The British also asked that, in return for a $56,000 payment, Curtiss supply its design studies and other pertinent information (e.g., wind tunnel data) on their XP-46 to the North American design team. The XP-46 was a descendant of the P-40. It had also been ordered for the RAF but was eventually canceled in 1941 after the two prototypes demonstrated inferior performance to the early P-47 Thunderbolt. One feature of the XP-46 that was shared by the NA-73 was an advanced radiator scoop design on the lower fuselage. The large scoop provided cooling air for both the ethylene glycol engine coolant and the engine oil. Hot waste air was vented out via a ramp in

Left and above: NAA engineers check out large scale models of the Mustang that were used for wind tunnel tests. These tests help perfect the aircraft's aerodynamic design, including the unconventional laminar flow airfoil of the wing. (Left, G. Balzer Collection; Above, Piet Collection)

Features of the Curtiss XP-46 contributed to the design of the Mustang. Most significant of these was the large air scoop and exhaust port for the radiators for the engine oil and glycol coolant mounted under the fuselage. The XP-46 never went into production. (NMUSAF)

the aft part of the scoop assembly. This venting would produce more thrust than the drag caused by the frontal cross section of the scoop.

Just how much Curtiss data was used in the NA-73 design is debatable. Curtiss protested that their design work had been entirely appropriated, while those at North American vehemently denied the claim. The truth is probably somewhere in between. On one hand, the NA-73 had much in common with the XP-46, but various North American features granted the NA-73 superior performance. On the other hand, it is hard to imagine the NA-73 engineered in such a short period of time without use of the Curtiss data. Further, it is also important to realize that the NA-73 was not conjured out of a vacuum. Ed Schmued had been informally working on fighter designs as early as 1934. Many features of what he considered to be an optimized fighter were already thoroughly worked out on paper.

On the other side of the coin, the incorporation of an innovative laminar flow wing was undeniably unique to the NA-73. When air encounters a moving object such as an airplane wing, air begins to flow over an airfoil in smooth, sheet-like (or laminar) layers. As the smooth airflow proceeds aft, it begins to break down into turbulent, chaotic eddies which produce drag through friction, and the wing becomes less efficient. By the late 1930s, wind tunnel tests demonstrated that wing shapes that reached their maximum thickness at various points farther aft of that of standard airfoils of the day preserved their laminar flow longer. Horkey, with the support of NACA, calculated and recalculated airfoil contours and pressure distributions to finally arrive at a wing that had a sixteen percent thickness/chord ratio at the wing root and eleven percent at the wingtip. Another challenge required wings that would be exceptionally

AS AIR MOVES OVER THE WING, CAUSING FRICTION, TURBULENCE IS PRODUCED, CAUSING DRAG

STANDARD AIRFOIL

THE LAMINAR AIRFOIL DELAYS FRICTION-CAUSING TURBULENCE, REDUCING DRAG

LAMINAR AIRFOIL

The design of the laminar airfoil is compared to that of the conventional airfoil in this illustration that shows how the drag-producing turbulent boundary layer air moved farther aft on the laminar airfoil. (Roszak)

smooth. Surface imperfections as small as 0.002 inches (e.g. rivets and panel lines) would compromise the laminar flow.

On September 9, 1940, the prototype was virtually complete and was formally designated as the NA-73X. Only 102 days had passed after the contract had been signed. The British named the new fighter "Mustang," intending to evoke qualities of the wild horse of the American West. The first production British version was to follow the NA-73X and was formally designated as the Mustang Mk. I. The Luftwaffe had just commenced their Blitz bombing campaign against England as the NA-73X was rolled out. A comparatively small force of Hurricanes and Spitfires engaged in the defense of England against the numerically superior Luftwaffe. Britain's need for fighters became increasingly desperate by the day.

Test pilot Vance Breese prepares to take the NA-73X into the air for its maiden flight on October 26, 1940. He flew the aircraft five more times, demonstrating the soundness of the design and its potential as a warplane. With sandbags being used to chock the wheels, the Allison engine is warmed up prior to the flight. Note the scoop for the radiators under the fuselage in the open position. (G. Balzer Collection)

The engine failed early into the seventh flight of the NA-73X in late November 1940. North American test pilot Paul Balfour tried to save the airplane and glide it back to Mines Field. Unable to make the runway, he dropped the gear and put the aircraft down in a farmer's field. The extended landing gear made the aircraft violently flip tail-over-nose. The NA-73X suffered extensive damage, and Balfour's life was saved only by the rollover structure located behind the pilot's seat. Instead of writing off the wrecked airframe, North American engineers immediately set out to repair the damage. (Both, G. Balzer Collection)

The NA-73X was ready for flight, but Allison was late in delivering the 1,120-horsepower Allison V-1710-39 powerplant. This engine was the third flight-worthy F-series engine produced and was installed in the NA-73X before Allison's formal testing of the engine began. Time was also lost when, upon delivery, it was discovered that a minor design change by Allison prevented attachment to the NA-73X's engine mounts. Nevertheless, the British Purchasing Commission ordered another 300 airframes at this time. NAA engineers solved the engine mounting issue, and twenty-eight days later engine and taxi tests commenced. North American hired freelance test pilot Vance Breese to fly the NA-73X. He took the aircraft aloft on its maiden flight on the morning of October 26, 1940, from the North American facility at Mines Field which today is part of Los Angeles International Airport. The NA-73X performed beyond expectations. Breese flew the airplane six more times and identified a range of manageable problems to correct.

Former Lockheed test pilot, Paul Balfour, was the first engineering test pilot to fly the NA-73X on November 20. This test hop was to be the first to explore the high-speed flight characteristics of the NA-73X. Balfour was complacent. He refused a routine check-out in the new airplane before his first flight. Twelve minutes after take-off, the engine failed. His unfamiliarity may have led to his failure to switch fuel tanks when the selected tank ran dry. However, the USAAF report on the incident blamed a flaw in the carburetor air intake design. Regardless, Balfour turned the airplane back towards Mines Field

to make a dead stick landing to save the NA-73X. Realizing that he would not make the runway, Balfour maneuvered to put the aircraft down in a freshly plowed bean field. He extended the landing gear instead of opting for a belly landing. As the wheels dug into the earth, the inertia at the back end of the plane violently flipped it tail-over-nose. Only the reinforced rollover structure behind the seat saved Balfour's life. The NA-73X had accumulated just three hours and twenty minutes of flight time.

The NA-73X was recovered and rebuilt, returning to flight six weeks later as Robert Chilton assumed the position of chief test pilot. It flew an additional thirty-seven flights and was retired on July 15, 1941, since production aircraft would by then serve as better flight test platforms. These included the first production Mustang Mk. I that remained in the United States and never went to England. Further, the crash of the NA-73X had no impact on the perception of the aircraft. The U.K. order increased to 620 airframes. The design was clearly a winner. Its performance was superior to the P-40 Warhawk which was the best single-engine fighter in the USAAF inventory at that time.

Manufacturing Early Mustangs

Mustang Mk. Is were manufactured as quickly as possible and sent to the Royal Air Force. Initial management work by Dutch Kindelberger and design work by Ed Schmued paid

North American began mass-production of Mustang Mk. Is for the RAF. By December 1941, they were completing three Mustang Mk. Is per day, with the number increasing substantially as production continued. The key to such high output involved a modular construction approach, where completed sub-assemblies, such as the fuselage, wings, and tail, were already completed when they were mated to all the other major components. (Both, G. Balzer Collection)

various dividends, including the idea for a modular manufacturing approach that allowed for high-output mass production. The North American production line continually increased its daily output of Mustang Mk. Is as production continued. The key to this capability involved the fuselage, tail section, wings, and landing gear systems built as independent components and then joined together as completed assemblies. Hydraulic, electrical, and control lines needed to be connected, and then the sub-assemblies were bolted together. This approach was established with the Mustang Mk. I, and it continued to the end of Mustang production.

The Mustang's fuselage sub-assembly came together by joining the engine mount section to the main fuselage section. The semi-monocoque fuselage was almost entirely composed of aluminum alloy, except for the stainless-steel engine firewall which also doubled as an armor plate for the pilot. The aircraft's oil tank, fuel booster pump, electrical connections, hydraulic system reservoir, and other gear were attached to various areas of the firewall. When the engine was added later, most of the work involved only the attachment of fittings. The cockpit section consisted of the two sidewalls, instrument panel, windscreen, radio shelf, side windows, and canopy. On the underside of the fuselage, the oil cooler/radiator assembly was added. The forward portion of the inlet was fabricated from Alclad aluminum alloy. Extensive use of Dzus fasteners in various areas allowed for quick and easy removal of panels for inspection and maintenance.

The tail sub-assembly started just aft of the engine/oil cooler radiator exhaust and included the tail wheel well, vertical stabilizer and rudder, and a left and right horizontal stabilizer and elevator assemblies. The horizontal stabilizers were built as a single unit. Each elevator had a lead mass balance integrated into their outboard leading edge. In the early Mustangs, elevators and the rudder were fabric-covered (Grade A mercerized cotton). Rudder and elevator operation was achieved using conventional control cables.

The Mustang's completed wing sub-assembly included the left and right wings joined together by a center section that also served as the cockpit floor. The wing sub-assembly included the main gear wells, machine gun and ammunition bays, and left and right ninety-gallon internal fuel tanks. The left and right hydraulically-powered wing flaps were between the fuselage and the ailerons and were skinned in aluminum. Likewise, the left and right ailerons were metal-covered but operated using conventional control cables. In a laminar flow wing, airflow will interact with features such as flush-mounted rivet heads and panel line gaps to create turbulence, and thus decrease aerodynamic efficiency. To ensure the smoothest laminar flow on these early Mustangs, all rivets and panel lines on the forward forty percent of the upper and lower wings were filled with a fast-drying red vellutine putty which was sanded smooth and then painted in a gray primer. The remaining sixty percent of the wing's surface was painted in a Zinc Chromate primer.

The left and right retractable main landing gear components were hydraulically actuated. The struts attached to the landing gear support castings inside the wing where they could pivot laterally. Each landing gear was a full-cantilevered shock strut with its axle bolted to the shock strut piston. Scissor-type torque links transmitted torque placed on the axle and fork into the shock strut cylinder. Each main gear was fitted with a disk brake system powered by an independent hydraulic system and attached to a wheel that was twenty-seven inches in diameter. The tail wheel assembly was also functionally a shock strut. It was retracted and extended using hydraulic power. The tail wheel was steerable using the rudder pedals and could swivel through 360 degrees. Toe pedals at the top of the rudder pedals controlled braking.

Procurement and Growth of the Early Mustang Lineage

Various written sources have perpetuated the myth that the USAAC had an initial lack of interest in the Mustang which fueled subsequent indecision to act in acquiring the airplane for American use. This is mostly incorrect. The NA-73 and Mustang Mk. I did have an uphill battle with key members of the Air Corps' leadership, but USAAC interest was concerted, serious, and focused where it actually mattered: with Lt. Benjamin Kelsey. His interest slowly spread to then Lt.Col. Ira Eaker. As stated earlier, Kelsey saw to it that two aircraft from the original British order were supplied to Wright Field, Ohio, for testing. His forward thinking did not stop there. Kelsey correctly perceived the potential of the new aircraft for the United States and was able to place an order for 150 aircraft designated as the "P-51" on July 7, 1941 shortly after the USAAC had been renamed as the United States Army Air Forces. This was even before the two prototype XP-51s arrived in Dayton. While it was a small order for the first American Mustangs, it was the most aircraft that budgetary realities could acquire at

Two Mustang Mk. Is from the British order were provided to the USAAF and sent to Wright Field, Ohio, for testing. These two aircraft were designated XP-51s. They had U. S. national insignias in all four wing positions, and U. S. ARMY was lettered in black under the wings. Note the original short carburetor scoop on top of the forward fuselage. (G. Balzer Collection)

The P-51-NA was the first production American Mustang. Although very similar to the previous Mustang Mk. I, they did away with the mixed battery of machine guns (including the chin-mounted units) and replaced them with two 20mm cannons in each wing. The USAAF received fifty-five P-51-NAs, and ninety-three went to the British who designated them as the Mustang Mk. IA. Two were retained to become testbeds for the Rolls-Royce Merlin engine. The F-6A reconnaissance variant was also based on the P-51-NA. (Piet Collection)

the time.

The P-51-NA (with no variant suffix letter) was nearly identical to the Mustang Mk. I. The only meaningful difference was the replacement of the mixed-caliber machine gun armament of the British version with four 20mm cannons. Ninety-three P-51s were sent to the Royal Air Force where they were called Mustang Mk. IAs. With this order from the U. S. Army, North American attached the nickname "Apache" for these U. S. aircraft. Yet, the British name, Mustang, had taken root, and it became the official name of the aircraft by USAAF directive.

Meanwhile, the first XP-51 arrived at Wright Field on August 24, 1941. The second airplane arrived on December 16, 1941. By then, the Japanese attack on Pearl Harbor had caused everything in the United States to change dramatically. No isolationist could still claim that this was just a war between Hitler and Churchill. It was noted by North American and the USAAF that the British had fitted some of their Mustang Mk. Is with cameras for use in the tactical reconnaissance role. As soon as P-51s became available, cameras were fitted to various airframes. Redesignated as F-6As, these reconnaissance aircraft would become the first U. S. Mustangs to see combat over North Africa.

Initial wartime budgets for pursuit aircraft rapidly increased. Priorities had to be established, and where fighters were concerned, top importance was given to producing large numbers of those already on production lines. This meant that quantity was more important than testing. Doing so would get more P-38s, P-39s, and P-40s into combat as quickly as possible. Further, even more resources had to be allocated to pilot and ground crew training. Meanwhile, the Navy needed more ships, the Army required more tanks and artillery pieces, and everyone needed more trained personnel. American P-51 production was not prioritized in this environment, so Lt. Kelsey came up with a way to creatively beat the system again and procure additional USAAF Mustangs.

Using remaining funds allocated for attack aircraft, Kelsey asked North American to quickly develop a dive bomber variant of the NA-73. It was designated as the A-36A, the next available attack aircraft designation. It was fitted with the Allison 1710-87 engine, optimized for low-altitude performance where dive bombers operate, and it had two underwing hardpoints for carrying bombs up to 500-pounds in size. Internal

Partially to sustain the American orders for Mustangs and partially to fulfill an ill-defined but very real need for ground attack aircraft, the A-36A dive bomber variant was developed from the P-51-NA. Its most distinctive features were the upper and lower wing-mounted dive brakes and the change to a six-machine gun configuration with two in the chin. Two hardpoints were added under the wings to carry bombs or external fuel tanks. (Piet Collection)

The lineage of Allison-powered Mustangs ended with the P-51A. These aircraft were essentially an A-36 without the dive brakes, and the two machine guns in the cowling were deleted. The engine was upgraded to the V-1710-81. A total of 310 were built, with fifty-five going to the RAF, and thirty-five of the USAAF P-51As being converted to F-6B reconnaissance aircraft. (G. Balzer Collection)

armament consisted of six .50-caliber machine guns; four in the wings and two chin-mounted in the nose, similar to the Mustang Mk. I. Dive flaps were added to both upper and lower surfaces of the wings. Kelsey ordered 500 of these dive bombers on April 16, 1942. The first A-36A rolled off the North American production lines in Inglewood in September 1942. The earlier North American name, "Apache," was commonly used for the A-36A, but it was never formally recognized by the U. S. Army Air Forces.

The next version of the Mustang to be produced was the P-51A-NA. It was fitted with the improved Allison V-1710-81 engine and was the last Mustang to have an Allison powerplant. Some features were carried over from the A-36, including underwing hardpoints for bombs or external fuel tanks, but the dive-bombing gear and chin-mounted machine guns were deleted. A total of 310 P-51As were built. Many of these were delivered directly to squadrons in the China-Burma-India (CBI) and Mediterranean Theaters. Another fifty were delivered to the RAF as Mustang Mk. IIs. Thirty-five others were fitted with cameras and designated F-6Bs.

Developing a Niche: Allison-Engined Mustangs Join the RAF

The first batch of operational Mustangs were approved for release to the RAF in August 1941, and by then procurement was managed through the Lend-Lease Act. The first aircraft reached Great Britain in October, delivered by ship to Liverpool. RAF evaluation involving several early Mustang Mk. Is followed at the Aeroplane and Armament Experimental Establishment (A&AEE) at Boscombe Down on Salisbury Plain in October 1942. They found the Mustang Mk. I could reach 375 mph at 15,000 feet, whereas the maximum speed of the top-of-the-line Spitfire Mk. V was 340 mph at the same altitude. In

a dive, the Mustang attained a speed of 500 mph while the engine provided power without strain. It was also more stable in a dive and had a superior roll rate to the Spitfire Mk. V. Above this altitude, it was outclassed by the Spitfire Mk. V and the German Bf 109F. The Mustang was also outclassed by the Fw 190A-3, except for its faster speed below 15,000 feet and its tighter turning radius.

The A&AEE trials found some faults which were corrected. Others, such as very poor rearward visibility, was something they had to live with. One problem that plagued early Mustangs involved the guns jamming when fired under negative G loads. It was also reasoned that the Mustang would be an excellent tactical reconnaissance platform. The poor high-altitude performance of the Mustang, along with the employment of the Spitfire in high-altitude regimes, helped the Mustang find its niche; close air support for "Army Co-Operation" involving air-to-air, air-to-ground, and reconnaissance roles.

During this period, more Mustangs began to arrive in England. Squadrons were outfitted, and pilot training commenced. Introduction to combat continued to be delayed. Before it could be deemed combat-ready, A&AEE had to progressively clear the Mustang across multiple performance milestones, and any modifications had to then be retroactively added to every Mustang that had already been delivered. One such feature was the addition of an F.24 camera fitting involving a new mount and canopy glazing.

The first combat sortie by an RAF Mustang Mk. I was an armed reconnaissance mission in early May 1942 over coastal France near Breck-sur-Mer. The RAF got their photos and destroyed a German flak tower at the cost of one Mustang. Ground attack missions began in July. RAF Mustangs eventually started to intrude into German airspace. They provided important intelligence, but their offensive activities amounted only to simple harassment. RAF Mustangs also began to es-

Following several long months of test and evaluation in England, Mustang Mk. Is finally became operational in July 1942. They flew low-level reconnaissance and ground attack missions along with serving as diversions for other missions. A Mustang Mk. 1A scored the type's first air-to-kill in August 1942. Their missions into France and Germany were at first little more than a source of nuisance to the Nazis, but tactics and targets evolved as RAF Mustangs later focused on hitting rail and port infrastructure targets. (G. Balzer Collection)

cort bombers and assist the Royal Navy with artillery spotting. The first Mustang air-to-air kill occurred on August 19th, 1942, during the Dieppe raid. There, an RAF airplane assigned to a Royal Canadian Air Force Squadron and flown by an American volunteer shot down an Fw 190.

Sporadic German raids into the south coast of England by Ju 88s and Fw 190s began to pick up in the early fall of 1942. Mustang Mk. I squadrons increasingly assumed patrol duties to counter the Luftwaffe, and by the summer of 1943, the raids ceased. RAF Mustangs then shifted to conducting three mission profiles: low-level sorties known as "Populars" (photo reconnaissance missions with a defined target), "Rhubarbs" (striking ground targets of opportunity), and "Rangers" (diversions designed to draw enemy attention away from other missions). Populars and Rubarbs were often flown at low level where they frequently encountered rather accurate German light anti-aircraft fire. The optimal altitude for the photography portion of a Popular mission was 900 feet. Over the first eighteen months of Rhubarb raids, the earlier harassment of the Germans gained greater focus. They began to specialize in locomotive-busting, critically damaging or destroying some 200 locomotives, over 200 barges, and an unknown number of German aircraft on the ground at a cost of only eight Mustangs. The aircraft's low- and medium-altitude performance was regarded as superlative, and at sea level, nothing could keep up with the Mustang. One British modification to the Allison V-1710 engine involved overboosting which involved either removing or resetting the engine's manifold pressure regulator. This pushed power output to 1,780 horsepower, or 210 horsepower greater than the manufacturer's design specifications.

Early American Mustangs in North Africa and the Mediterranean

By the late summer and fall of 1942, USAAF operational test and evaluation trials of three P-51s and three A-36s were conducted at Eglin Field, Florida. Subsequent reports applauded the P-51's handling, stability, and speed. It was declared as the best low-level American fighter. Various improvements and the need for an engine to allow for sufficient performance above 15,000 feet were also called for in these reports, but by then it was known that a Merlin-powered variant

was on the way. The A-36 was similarly praised, but it was generally considered to be an inferior dive bomber, because it was simply too fast, even when using its dive brakes. Concerns over excessive wing loading and structural failure led to directives prohibiting dive brake use, but they were clearly used operationally.

The first American Mustangs to see combat were F-6As and A-36s that began to arrive in North Africa four months after Operation Torch commenced. The 111th and 154th Tactical Reconnaissance Squadrons received their first F-6As and A-36s in March 1943. The A-36 could also be fitted with cameras. Soon, they were flying combat reconnaissance missions into Tunisia providing critical battlefield intelligence that was valuable for planning by Generals Montgomery and Patton.

Following the Allied victory in North Africa, the invasion of Sicily and Italy were next. Preparations for the assault saw the 111th flying recon sorties around the clock, and they were later joined by A-36s of the 27th and 86th Fighter-Bomber Groups. The first mission of the Italian campaign was flown by an A-36 on June 6, 1943. In the early phases of the battle, A-36s could not keep up with the demand for their services. While the USAAF trials at Eglin Field gave the A-36 poor marks as a dive

The first American Mustangs to fly combat missions were F-6As during the North African Campaign. After North Africa was secured, they continued to provide valuable photographic intelligence as the Allies moved into Sicily and finally to Italy. Here, a photographic specialist installs a camera in an F-6A prior to a mission over Italy. (NMUSAF)

During the summer and fall of 1942, American P-51s and A-36As were tested at Eglin Field, Florida, prior to the types being sent into combat with American units. The A-36 received high marks for its speed and maneuverability, but it was actually considered too fast to be an effective dive bomber. Nevertheless, it served well in that role operationally. (NMUSAF)

Evaluations with the three P-51-NAs at Eglin Field resulted in the Mustang receiving excellent marks for its handling, speed, and maneuverability. It was rated as the best American low-level fighter. The need for a different engine that would deliver better performance at altitudes above 15,000 feet was again noted in the evaluations, but this was something that was already known, and work had already begun to develop a high-altitude variant. In fact, two P-51-NAs had been set aside to serve as test aircraft with the Rolls Royce Merlin engine that would power the high-altitude versions that would soon go into production. (NMUSAF)

No less than 150 mission markings are painted on the nose of this A-36A assigned to the 27th Fighter Bomber Group. The photograph was taken at Gela, Sicily, in late 1943. A-36As and P-51As played a major part in the North African campaign and in the invasions of Sicily and Italy. (NMUSAF)

bomber, pilots at the squadron level worked out the optimal techniques and tactics to capitalize on the Mustang's inherent capacity as a very accurate and survivable dive bomber.

The invasion of Sicily began on July 10, 1943. A-36s of the 27th and 86th Fighter-Bomber Groups bombed and strafed rail yards, ships, fuel and oil dumps, depots, factories, troop encampments, bridges, and gun emplacements. Then, F-6As of the 111th Observation Squadron and three RAF Mustang squadrons (including a few A-36s loaned from the USAAF) followed up to conduct bomb damage assessment. During this time, pilots and crews started to call the A-36 the "Invader" but this nickname did not go beyond their squadrons. Missions began to be flown from forward operating bases, and when Sicily fell, focus shifted to targets in Italy itself. The A-36 also began to accumulate air-to-air kills. On August 22, A-36s of the 527th FBS were assigned to escort a B-26 mission, and this led to aerial victories over five Bf 109s and C.202s while no B-26s were lost. The first Mustang ace was an A-36 pilot!

As the main invasion force reached Italy on September 9, A-36As provided close air support until sundown. Days later, they strafed and destroyed at least ten Ju 88s preparing to take off and bomb the Allied beachhead. In another attack a few days later, more than a dozen Bf 109s were destroyed on the ground at an airfield south of Rome. Soon thereafter, 527th FBS pilots broke up what would have been a lethal German counterattack on Allied forces. An A-36 sortie in October hit a massive Axis ammunition dump. The resulting explosion likely approached the kiloton range with the shockwave crushing in the skin and bending bulkheads of the A-36 closest to the detonation. The pilot managed to return to base, but that aircraft never flew again.

Throughout October and November 1943, A-36s (now part of the newly organized Fifteenth Air Force) contributed to the systematic erosion of German forces. The destruction wrought by A-36s far outweighed their losses, but since North American production had moved on to the P-51A, new replacement A-36s were not forthcoming. This generated growing operational strain, such that P-40s were brought into the squadrons

of the 86th FBG to offset A-36 losses. The pilots and aircraft soldiered on with their A-36s thoroughly involved at Anzio and Monte Cassino into March 1944. The A-36 also picked up a new mission, that of supply drops to ground forces. Rations and other needed supplies were stuffed into external fuel tanks that had been converted into supply canisters. By the end of the fight around Cassino in May, 86th FBG pilots had destroyed or damaged several hundred German vehicles, and they continued to relentlessly pound retreating Nazi forces. The last operational A-36s were transferred to the 111th TRS who still had plenty of reconnaissance work awaiting. The 525th transitioned to the P-47 Thunderbolt in June 1944, with pilots aware that they were losing their precision dive bombing capability which they had uniquely mastered.

Early Mustangs in the China-Burma-India Theater

In 1942, the Japanese threatened to take over key sections of China, Burma, and India in southern Asia. Their success would be disastrous for the Allies on many levels. When Burma was overrun, the Tenth Air Force was organized and based in India. One year later they were joined by the Fourteenth Air Force based in China. The build-up of fighter forces in the CBI theater saw the arrival of P-38s, P-40s, A-36s, and P-51As beginning in September 1943. Within the Tenth Air Force's 311th Fighter-Bomber Group, the 528th and 529th Fighter-Bomber Squadrons were equipped with A-36s, and the 530th FBS received P-51As. The 23rd Fighter Group was the heir to the "Flying Tigers" and started replacing their P-40 Warhawks with P-51As in November 1943.

The first Mustangs to see action in the CBI were 311th FBG A-36s in October 1943 over Myanmar. They bombed and strafed targets mostly in support of British ground forces but also flew numerous reconnaissance and support missions. The 23rd Fighter Group entered combat over China one month later with attacks on airfields, ports, rail yards, and shipping in mainland China, as well as reconnaissance flights and raids over Taiwan. The Mustang's long range was further extended

Ground crew personnel perform engine maintenance on P-51A, S/N 43-6151, which was assigned to Major Robert T. Smith of the 1st ACG in China. This P-51A was named "Barbie," and a color photo of Major Smith with it is in the P-51A section of the variants chapter. It was common practice to tape over the gun ports in each wing to prevent foreign matter from getting into the muzzles of the machine guns. (Piet Collection)

by external fuel tanks. This opened a new role, that of bomber escort. The aircraft quickly developed a reputation as a first-rate medium-altitude escort, complementing high-altitude P-38 patrols. P-51s were vital companions for bombers and the transport aircraft flying "The Hump" over the Himalayas from India to China. These diverse missions continued into the early spring of 1944, degrading Japanese forces in Burma and China. Up until this point, the Mustang had been conceived of as a close air support and ground attack aircraft, but the growing number of kills of Japanese fighters and bombers in the CBI began to change that perception.

The two squadrons of the 1st Air Commando Group (ACG) received thirty P-51As and began combat operations in February 1944. The independence granted to this special operations group allowed them to be more unconventional, hard-hitting, flexible, and effective than standard squadrons. This managerial approach was particularly effective in their support of the Chindits, the combined British-Indian ground force operating behind Japanese lines in Burma. March 1944 saw the Japanese invade India via northern Burma. While all Mustangs in range defended against the attack, the 1st ACG crippled the Japanese with highly aggressive counterattacks on Japanese airfields, supply routes, and communications while also conducting vital battlefield reconnaissance. They destroyed (mostly on the ground) up to twenty-five percent of all Japanese aircraft in Burma between February and April. The group was awarded a Distinguished Unit Citation for these acts. The 1st ACG experimented with the M10 "Bazooka" triple-tube rocket launchers, while another field modification involved a 450-foot-long cable attached to their bomb racks used to sever telegraph and telephone wires.

USAAF and RAF Allison-Powered Mustangs Over Europe, 1943-1945

American P-51s were a relative late-comer to the European Theater. Most of that history is dominated by USAAF P-51Bs, P-51Cs, P-51Ds, and P-51Ks. The lack of U. S. Allison-powered Mustangs in Europe is due in part because of its poor high-altitude performance. Most of the work they could have done involved the escort of high-altitude bombers. Since Allison-powered Mustangs would not stand much of a chance against Bf 109s and Fw 190s in that setting, they were never really considered for the role. At first, the USAAF erroneously believed that bombers did not need escorts, because the bombers' defensive armament would provide sufficient protection. Once the need for fighter escort was established, tactics initially limited their ability to leave the bomber formations

and engage the Luftwaffe. These tactics were changed when General Eaker was replaced by General Jimmy Doolittle in December 1943. By that time, the P-51B/C was arriving in theater for the USAAF and RAF, and it served as escorts where Allison-engined Mustangs dare not tread.

Yet, Allison-powered Mustangs were neither completely absent nor obsolete following the arrival of the Merlin-powered variants. F-6B reconnaissance aircraft, flown by the 67th Tactical Reconnaissance Group, began operating in England just before Christmas 1943. The group carefully developed their methods following the best practices of the RAF. The 67th TRG was tasked with a top-secret assignment to provide complete photographic coverage of the beaches and coastal regions of northwest France to be used in the planning for the Allied invasion of Europe. They were also joined by RAF and RCAF Mustangs in this work between February and March 1944. RAF Mustangs continued pressing their assaults on Nazi-occupied Europe. Of note were two squadrons of Mustang Mk. Is that conducted "Noball" missions, locating and attacking V-1 and V-2 launch sites beginning in early 1944. They also used their speed to intercept V-1s before they could hit their targets in England.

On D-Day, American F-6Bs of the 67th TRG were real-time "eyes in the sky" for the landings, looking for anything that could pose difficulties for the ground forces and their advance into the French countryside. RAF Mk. IA and Mk. II Mustangs (along with Spitfires and Seafires) directed British naval artillery onto their targets. F-6Bs and Mustang Mk. IIs provided photo intelligence in August that helped the Allies annihilate four German armored divisions in the Falaise Pocket. Less than a month later, an RCAF Mustang took the photos documenting a major German presence around Arnhem which infamously went unheeded before Operation Market Garden. Number 26 Squadron was equipped with the Mustang Mk. I from the beginning to the end. They were the first operator of the Mustang Mk. I, and fittingly they flew the last combat mission of an Allison-powered Mustang.

Analysis and Legacy of the Early Mustangs

Numerous accounts and contemporary narratives about the development and career of the early Mustangs portray them as an aircraft that had yet to meet its potential. Another notion holds that the introduction of the P-51D made early Mustangs instantaneously obsolete. It has also been casually but widely stated that the Allison V-1710 represented an aircraft-powerplant mismatch with early Mustangs. Others have asserted that the poor high-altitude performance of the

Allison engine was a surprise or a shocking disappointment to the British and USAAF. These are all myths disconnected from reality.

A far-reaching mystique surrounds the P-51D, and rightly so. Yet, an unfortunate side effect of this involves a diminished perception of all the Mustangs that preceded the -D model. Not all past writers have given early Mustangs the credit which they earned. Objective analysis shows Allison-powered Mustangs were excellent low- and medium-altitude fighters. Engineers of the day had more than sufficient knowledge of powerplants. Even before the flight of the NA-73X, it was well known and understood that the Allison engine-supercharger combination would produce a drop in performance above 15,000 feet.

It was envisioned that Allison-powered Mustangs would be low-level fighters, and later Packard Merlin-powered P-51Bs and P-51Cs would be the high-altitude versions. It is important to note that Mustangs with the Allison engine outperformed Merlin-powered variants below 15,000 feet, and no writer has ever criticized the Allison-powered early Mustangs for having poor performance at low altitudes. In the postwar air racing scene, Allison-engined Mustangs were universally preferred over Merlin-equipped airframes. They were not just faster on the deck, but the Allison engines were mechanically more reliable. When one reads the widespread claim the Merlin engine is what allowed the Mustang to reach its "potential," this is true only if high-altitude performance is considered. A more balanced and realistic assessment would be that both the Allison and Merlin-powered versions performed very well at the altitudes at which they were optimized. The Allison V-1710 was clearly the better engine for early Mustangs in the low- and medium-altitude fighter role.

The combat record of Allison-powered Mustangs must also be considered. Beginning with their introduction into RAF service, the Mustang's range and firepower were certainly effective at harassing the enemy within their territory. The sheer speed of the aircraft at low altitude led to its rapid adaptation to a tactical reconnaissance role where it literally shaped the outcome of campaigns such as the Battle of Tunis where photos taken by F-6s helped bring the North African conflict to a close. The performance of the P-51-NA, P-51A, and A-36A in the Mediterranean and CBI theaters underscores their success as what we today call a multi-role fighter. Mustangs were not just holding their own but defeating the most advanced Axis aircraft, then hitting ground or surface targets on the same mission. It was not just the Mustang's versatility, but its effectiveness that allowed it to achieve such success. Its capability and precision in close air support and dive bombing was lauded by Allied ground forces. The outcomes of the battles for Sicily and Italy were significantly shaped by Allison-powered Mustangs. The extensive destruction wrought upon Japanese forces in the CBI Theater (with the record of the 1st Air Commando Group as an example) further attests to the outsized impact of early Allison-powered Mustangs. One could argue that the Allison-powered Mustang in the Mediterranean and Far East was the A-10 Thunderbolt II of its era.

Some 300 P-51s can be found around the world today, either as museum pieces or as flyable airframes. Of these, only nine are Allison-engined early Mustangs. One of the two XP-51s is preserved at the EAA Museum in Oshkosh, Wisconsin, and a P-51A has been recently backdated to represent the NA-73X. Three A-36s survive, two of which are flyable. Four P-51A-10-NA aircraft still exist, and two are airworthy. These survivors are all based in the United States and can sometimes be seen in airshow performances, helping keep alive the memories of their pilots and their crews, of their valiant deeds, and of those who made the ultimate sacrifice in the defense of freedom. Now more than eighty years after its first flight, Allison-powered early Mustangs can clearly be seen in terms of their unique contributions by helping shape the eventual collapse of Axis forces in North Africa and Italy while also stemming the expansion of Japan into Central Asia.

One of the few remaining Allison-engined Mustangs still in existence is this P-51A, S/N 43-6251, that is owned by Planes of Fame at Chino, California. Presently it is painted to represent "Mrs. Virginia" that flew with the 1st Air Commando Group. One change that has been made to the aircraft is that the navigation lights on the wings are the later type that were mounted directly on the wing tips, which first appeared on the P-51D variant. Operational P-51As had the two-light arrangement on each wing, with one light on top of the wing and one on the bottom. (Manning).

MAIN DIFFERENCES TABLE -- ALLISON-ENGINED MUSTANG VARIANTS

NAA MODEL	NA-73X	NA-73 & NA-83	NA-91	NA-97	NA-99
U.S. DESIGNATION	NONE	XP-51	P-51-NA	A-36A	P-51A
BRITISH DESIGNATION	NONE	MUSTANG Mk. I	MUSTANG Mk. IA	NONE	MUSTANG Mk. II
ARMAMENT	NONE	2 X .50-CAL. MG IN CHIN + 2 X .50-CAL. & 4 X .303-CAL. MG IN WINGS	4 X 20mm CANNON IN WINGS	2 X .50-CAL. MG IN CHIN + 4 X .50-CAL MG IN WINGS	4 X .50-CAL MG IN WINGS
ALLISON ENGINE	V-1710-39	V-1710-39	V-1710-V-39	V-1710-87	V-1710-81
CARBURETOR SCOOP	THIN & SHORT ON TOP OF NOSE	THIN & LONG ON TOP OF NOSE	THIN & LONG ON TOP OF NOSE	THICK & LONG ON TOP OF NOSE	THICK & LONG ON TOP OF NOSE
COOLING AIR SCOOP	SHALLOW & HINGED	SHALLOW & HINGED	SHALLOW & HINGED	SHALLOW & FIXED	SHALLOW & FIXED
LANDING/TAXI LIGHTS	SINGLE LIGHT ON EACH WING	SINGLE LIGHT ON EACH WING	SINGLE LIGHT ON EACH WING	TWO LIGHTS IN ONE UNIT ON LEFT WING	SINGLE LIGHT ON LEFT WING
PROPELLER	CURTISS ELECTRIC 3-BLADE 10-' 6" DIAMETER	CURTISS ELECTRIC 3-BLADE 10' 6" (EARLY) 10' 9" (LATE)	CURTISS ELECTRIC 3-BLADE 10' 9" DIAMETER	CURTISS ELECTRIC 3-BLADE 10' 9" DIAMETER	CURTISS ELECTRIC 3-BLADE 10' 9" DIAMETER
PITOT PROBE	L-SHAPED UNDER RIGHT WING	L-SHAPED UNDER RIGHT WING	L-SHAPED UNDER RIGHT WING	BOOM STYLE ON RIGHT WING	L-SHAPED UNDER RIGHT WING
NUMBER BUILT	1	620	150	500	310

There were a number of specific physical differences between the Allison-powered Mustang variants. An understanding of these differences is important. While these differences are covered in the text and captions of this publication, this table summarizes those differences in order to present a side-by-side comparison of these variants, so that they can be studied and compared on a single page.

A Mustang Mk. IA, painted in a gray and green camouflage scheme, awaits its next mission while assigned to an RAF tactical reconnaissance group. Note that this Mustang Mk. 1A has a circular section cut out of its right rear cockpit window to allow use of a camera mounted in that area. This is unusual, because most camera windows were mounted on the left side. The photo is not reversed, as indicated by the presence of the three small vents on the forward fuselage in front of the windscreen. These vents were only on the right side of the fuselage. (Piet Collection)

ALLISON-ENGINED MUSTANG DIMENSIONS

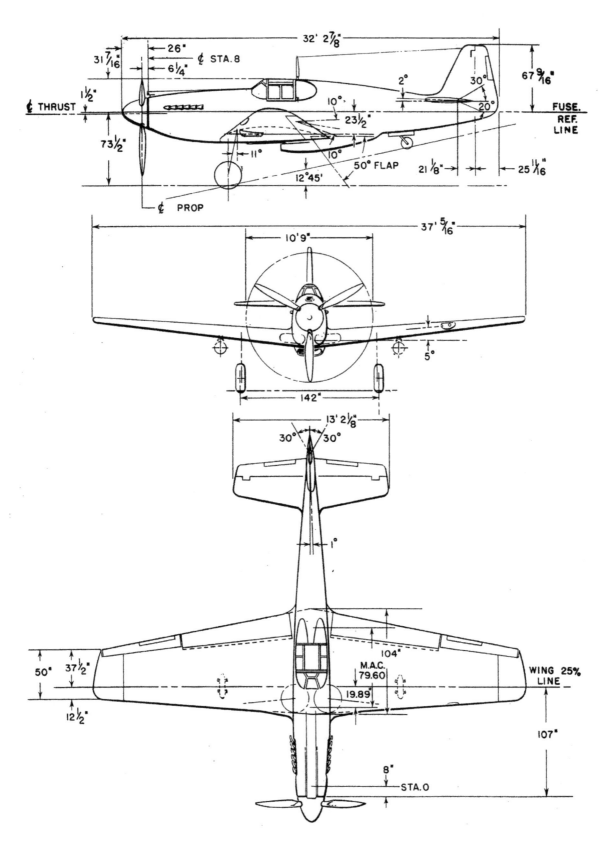

Taken from the A-36A erection and maintenance manual, this drawing provides the important dimensions for the aircraft. Although the drawing is of the A-36A, the dimensions stated are the same for all Allison-powered Mustangs. (NMUSAF)

ALLISON-ENGINED MUSTANG VARIANTS
NA-73X

The NA-73X represented the origin of the entire lineage of North American Aviation's Mustang aircraft. This single prototype was built by hand between May 30 and September 9, 1940. Twenty variants or derivatives would emerge with the NA-73X as their ancestor, from the celebrated P-51D to the F-82 Twin Mustang of the 1950s, and then to the Piper PA-48 Enforcer which completed its flight test program in 1984. The NA-73X is immediately recognizable as a Mustang, because the basic shape of the aircraft changed very little over time. The fairing for one of the chin-mounted machine guns is visible just below the spinner in this early photograph, although no weapons were ever installed in the aircraft. The locations for the wing guns were simply painted in black on the wings. Note the L-shaped pitot probe under the right wing. This would remain standard on all future Mustang variants except for the A-36A. (G. Balzer Collection)

As soon as the British signed the contract with North American Aviation on April 10, 1940, work immediately began on the single prototype that would be the sire of the entire line of Mustangs. Designated Model NA-73X at North American, this airframe would be rolled out 102 days later, still waiting for its Allison engine. The fundamental lines and configuration of the NA-73X would see relatively little in the way of changes on all subsequent single-engine Mustang variants.

The NA-73X was given the civil registry of NX19998, and it possessed several unique features. Specific aspects of its shape were somewhat different than production Mustangs. The nose of the NA-73X was shorter and the original short

Three distinctive features of the NA-73X are noticeable in this photograph. These include the frameless blown windscreen, the stepped trailing edge on the outer main landing gear doors, and the tube-style exhaust ports for the engine. The addition of what may be an air inlet tube just forward of the exhaust ports appeared when it returned to flight in early 1941 after being repaired following the emergency landing accident. Note also the thin whip antenna on the spine above the cockpit. When the prototype was rebuilt, the fairings for the nose guns were removed, as were the painted openings for the wing guns. (NAA via Piet)

As the NA-73X banks in flight, details on the underside are revealed. The aircraft's civil registry, NX19998, was lettered in black beneath the left wing. Note the red, white, and blue markings added to the rudder. (NAA via Piet)

carburetor air scoop was atop the engine cowling. The radiator air scoop was short and more curved along the underside. A hinged upper and lower mouth of the radiator scoop delivered air to the oil and engine coolant radiators. These were two distinct units in the NA-73X. The upper lip of the radiator scoop sat flush on the underside of the wing, and this led to the radiator ingesting choppy boundary layer air. The NA-73X also had a one-piece, racing-style, blown windscreen with no framework. This was a feature that was unique to the prototype that would be replaced with a framed bulletproof design on production aircraft. Although it was never armed, fairings for the chin-mounted .50-caliber machine guns and painted "holes" for the wing guns were initially present on the completed aircraft, although they were later removed. The outer doors for the main landing gear had a unique shape with a small trailing edge step. The wheels were originally ones taken from a T-6 Texan.

Once the Allison V-1710-39 engine arrived and was installed in the aircraft, taxi tests began. On October 26, 1940, Vance Breese lifted off the runway from Mines Field in Los Angeles for a maiden flight lasting five minutes. Flight test results immediately demonstrated a sound aircraft, and confirmed that North American had made good on its promise to build a fighter that would outperform the Curtiss P-40 while using the same powerplant.

As described in the history chapter, the Allison V-1710-39 engine quit during the eighth test flight and the aircraft suffered significant damage when it flipped over onto its back following a wheels-down emergency landing in a soft field. By this time, it had production-style wheels. The NA-73X was repaired and returned to flight six weeks later as the first production Mustang Mk. I joined the flight test program. The repaired NA-73X had a few additional changes. The nose gun fairings were removed and faired over. A small tube was fitted forward of the exhaust ports on the left side that may have been an engine cooling air inlet. The rudder was later painted with the US-AAC's red, white, and blue colors. By July 1941, it made sense to retire the NA-73X, because early production airframes were better suited as flight test aircraft. The final disposition of the sole NA-73X is unclear. It may have been stripped and then donated to a technical school in the Los Angeles area, but from there it disappeared from history.

MUSTANG Mk. I

The Mustang Mk. I was the first variant of the Mustang to go into production. Once completed, Mustang Mk. Is were flown by North American on a check-out flight. During this flight, American national insignias were usually in six positions, but the British serial number was lettered in black on each side of the aft fuselage. The serial, AL958, on this aircraft indicates that it was the first Mustang Mk. I in the second production batch. (NAA via Piet)

On May 29, 1940, the British placed an order for 320 aircraft which it designated the Mustang Mk. I, also known by the North American design designation NA-73. These aircraft were assigned the British serial numbers AG345 through AG664. A second order for an additional 300 Mustang Mk. Is in three more production batches spanned serial numbers AL958 through AL999, AM100 through AM257, and AP164 through AP263.

For the most part, this first production variant differed little from the NA-73X. A framed, 1.5-inch-thick bulletproof windscreen replaced the distortion-prone blown windscreen on the prototype. Inside the cockpit, the control column featured the British style circular hand grip at the top with the trigger button for the guns at the 11 o'clock position. The instrument panel featured a few RAF-specific features, such as the compass (though some did have U. S. compasses) and the IFF and VHF radio gear. An initial configuration had two IFF antenna wires running between the sides of the fuselage to the tips of the horizontal stabilizers. This was soon replaced by one antenna between the aft cockpit and the vertical stabilizer cap. Cockpit heating and cooling features were introduced. Windscreen de-icing was first accomplished using hot engine bleed air, but midway through the first production run, a glycol-based system was adopted. Cockpit lighting and formation lights (to illuminate the upper wings) were added.

The carburetor intake scoop on top of the nose was lengthened to a point just aft of the spinner beginning with the fourth production Mustang Mk. I. This alteration was retrofitted to the

The very first Mustang Mk. I, S/N AG345, was nearing completion when this photograph was taken. Note the original short carburetor scoop on top of the forward fuselage. At this time, the British serial number was painted in small letters and numbers on the rudder. (NAA via Piet)

Once completed, AG345 was rolled out for a publicity photograph while still in a natural metal finish. No armament had been installed at this time. Note that the serial number is painted in large black letters and numbers under the left wing in much the same way the civil registration letters and numbers had been painted under the left wing of the NA-73X. Interestingly, the main gear wheels have covers on them. (NAA via Piet)

first three Mustang Mk. Is as well, given its possible role in the crash of the NA-73X. The most significant cosmetic change involved the radiator unit. The mouth of the radiator unit itself was lowered and was offset from the wing to eliminate the boundary air ingestion issue. Mustang Mk. Is retained only the lower hinged radiator scoop which could be opened for increased cooling during engine run-ups and taxiing, while the exit flap was modified into a movable unit to prevent excessive cooling. The addition of self-sealing fuel tanks was the final major difference between the prototype and these first production airframes. As was the case with the NA-73X, the Mustang Mk. I had a single landing/taxi light installed in the leading edge of each wing.

The British wanted a heavily armed fighter with a mixed battery of eight machine guns. Two .50-caliber guns were mounted beneath the engine in the nose section, while the other two .50-caliber guns and the four .303-caliber weapons were in the wings, mounted outside the arc of the propeller.

The first flight of a Mustang Mk. I took place on April 23, 1941. The first example joined the repaired NA-73X in the flight test and evaluation program. Contractual arrangements with the British called for two Mustang Mk. Is to be turned over to the USAAC for test and evaluation.

The Mustang Mk. I began service with the RAF in July 1942, and it promptly demonstrated that it could outperform any other British or German fighter below 15,000 feet. Its only limitation was its service ceiling. Nevertheless, plans were al-

ready underway to develop high-altitude versions of the fighter with a different engine and supercharger combination.

By the time the Mustang Mk. I entered service with the RAF, the Battle of Britain had been won, and an invasion by Germany was no longer an imminent threat. Taking advantage of the speed and maneuverability of the aircraft, the British were the first to install a camera in a Mustang and use it in the tactical photographic-reconnaissance role. It was initially a field modification where a circular hole was cut in the aft left fuselage glazing. An F.24 camera was mounted behind the pilot on a rig attached to the aft fuselage decking. Mustang Mk. I photo ships initially only had this one camera. The second vertical camera aft of the radiator was developed by the U. S., and it was later added to select Mustang Mk. Is and Mk. IAs.

The NA-83 design represented a minor mid-production upgrade but was still designated Mustang Mk. I. These aircraft were intended to be armed with four Hispano 20mm cannons. Production delays made the cannons unavailable, so all NA-83s went to war with the standard Mustang Mk. I armament. The principal changes involved tropicalizing the aircraft for desert operations as per an RAF request. The NA-83 design also featured a slightly redesigned carburetor air scoop as later seen on the P-51A, A-36, and Mustang Mk. 1A. Other minor refinements included deletion of the formation lights, improvements to the hydraulic system, and the gun camera moved from the wing to the lower engine cowling.

AG345 was later painted in the standard RAF brown and green camouflage scheme with British roundels; however, this appearance is deceiving. It was painted as such for press photos, but it went directly into service with NAA's Mustang flight test program where it joined the rebuilt NA-73X. It appears to have remained in the United States for its entire service life. By the time this photo was taken, the longer carburetor scoop had been fitted, and the machine guns were installed. (NAA via Piet)

MUSTANG Mk. I

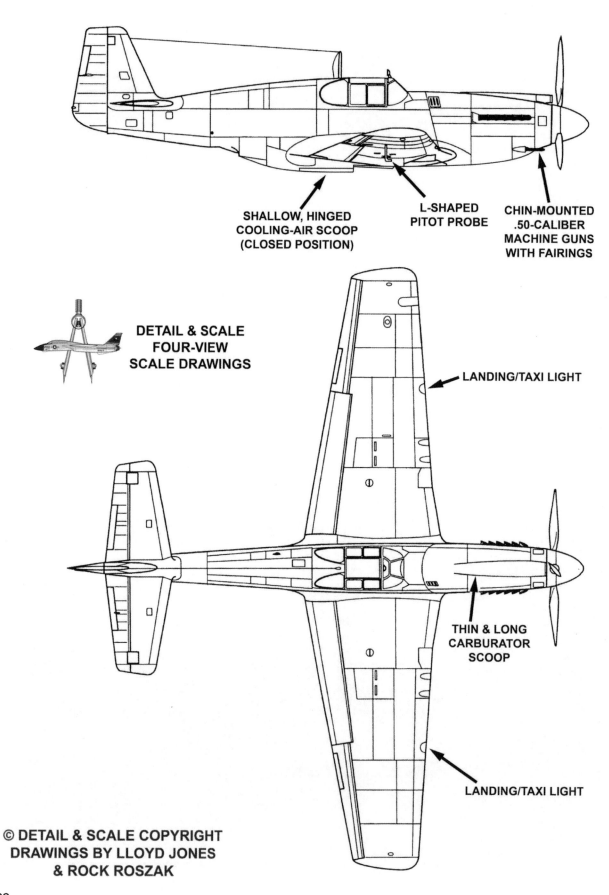

SHALLOW, HINGED
COOLING-AIR SCOOP
(CLOSED POSITION)

L-SHAPED
PITOT PROBE

CHIN-MOUNTED
.50-CALIBER
MACHINE GUNS
WITH FAIRINGS

DETAIL & SCALE
FOUR-VIEW
SCALE DRAWINGS

LANDING/TAXI LIGHT

THIN & LONG
CARBURATOR
SCOOP

LANDING/TAXI LIGHT

© DETAIL & SCALE COPYRIGHT
DRAWINGS BY LLOYD JONES
& ROCK ROSZAK

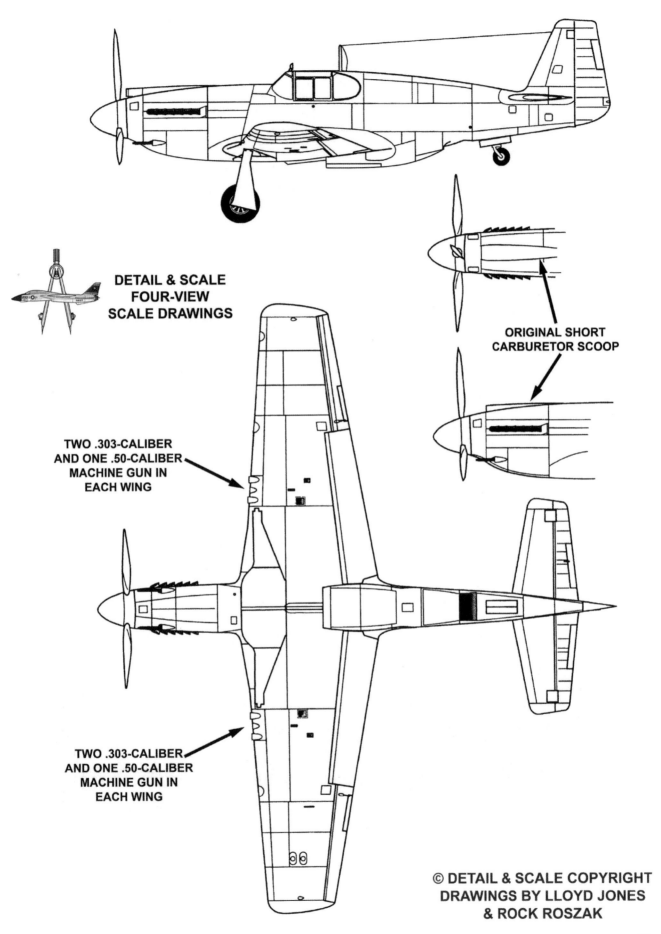

**DETAIL & SCALE
FOUR-VIEW
SCALE DRAWINGS**

TWO .303-CALIBER
AND ONE .50-CALIBER
MACHINE GUN IN
EACH WING

ORIGINAL SHORT
CARBURETOR SCOOP

TWO .303-CALIBER
AND ONE .50-CALIBER
MACHINE GUN IN
EACH WING

Above: Mustang Mk. Is were armed with eight machine guns. Six were in the wings, with each wing having a single .50-caliber machine gun flanked by two .303-caliber weapons. Two .50-caliber machine guns were mounted in the cowling beneath the engine. The cowl-mounted machine guns were arranged in a staggered configuration with the left machine gun barrel extending farther forward than the right. The arrangement of the three machine guns in the left wing is visible in the background to the right. (G Balzer Collection)

Right: Two newly completed Mustang Mk. Is of the first production batch share the ramp with B-25 Mitchell medium bombers at the North American plant in California, painted in their brown and green camouflage scheme. The cowl guns with their fairings are clearly visible. Note also the colors of the landing gear. The struts and wheels are silver, as are the inside surfaces of the gear doors. Early Mustang Mk. Is were fitted with a Curtiss Electric 3-blade propeller that was originally 10 feet, 6 inches in diameter, but during production the diameter was increased to 10 feet, 9 inches. (NAA via Piet)

Several details of the Mustang Mk. I are visible in this close-up of the canopy area. Noteworthy are the mast for the antenna wire, and that there is no wire that runs down vertically from the main wire into the radio compartment area. Just aft of the mast is a navigation light, and aft of it are two small vents for the radio compartment. These vents were on some, but not all, Mustang Mk. Is. On USAAF Mustangs, these vents were farther aft and on the sides of the fuselage. The small post forward of the windscreen has a tiny bead on the top that serves as the aiming point for the backup ring-and-bead gunsight. (NAA via Piet)

Mustang Mk. Is, and all subsequent Allison-engined Mustangs provided to the Royal Air Force, had the British style control column fitted with the circular hand grip at the top including its trigger button for the guns at the 11 o'clock position on the grip. (G. Balzer Collection)

This profile of the third production Mustang Mk. I illustrates how the aircraft looked after its check-out flight, and it was ready for delivery to the RAF. Mustang Mk. Is were delivered in a brown and green camouflage scheme, and after the check-out flight, the American insignias were painted over by British roundels in all six positions. Initially, the fin flash had three equal segments of red, white, and blue, front to rear. Note that the roundels on the fuselage were different from those on the wings. (Roszak)

Once in service, squadrons usually added a fuselage band and also painted the spinner with a squadron color. One or more letters on the fuselage indicated squadron assignment or the aircraft identification within the squadron. Note also how the serial number, AP247, was painted on this Mustang Mk. I at a slight angle, high in the fuselage band. The serial number indicates that this aircraft was in the fourth and final batch of Mustang Mk. Is to come off the production line. By this time, the British had changed to a different fin flash, as seen on this aircraft. The white center section of the flash was much thinner than the red and blue segments on either side. The style of the roundel on the fuselage had also changed. (Roszak)

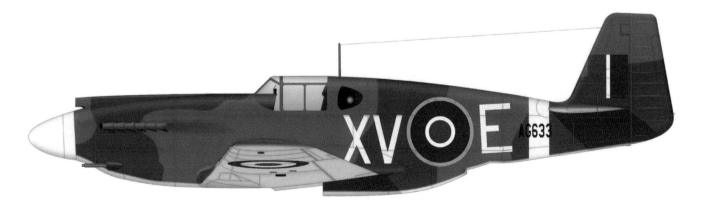

The British repainted some Mustang Mk. Is (and subsequent Mustang variants) in a gray and green camouflage scheme, particularly those used for photographic-reconnaissance missions. The XV in the fuselage code indicates that this Mustang Mk. I was assigned to Number 2 Squadron. (Roszak)

XP-51

The two XP-51s evaluated by the U. S. Army were originally the fourth and tenth Mustang Mk. Is to come off the production lines at North American. They were assigned U. S. serial numbers 41-038 and 41-039. As originally received by the USAAC, they retained the British armament, but the Americans were not happy with the mixed battery of machine guns, and this would be changed to four 20mm cannons in production P-51-NAs. (G. Balzer Collection)

When the Anglo-French Purchasing Commission arrived in the United States in early 1940, they were in desperate need of fighter aircraft. While the American deficit in fighters was not as grave as that faced by England in 1940, the U. S. military also had its problems. There was a shortage of personnel, and the ever-present lack of funding persisted, despite war clouds on the horizon. So, when the British contracted with North American to build the Mustang Mk. I, it was stipulated that two of the aircraft would be turned over to the U. S. Army Air Corps for evaluation. Thus, the British paid for these two aircraft for the United States.

Designated XP-51s (and still designated as the NA-73 by North American), the fourth and tenth production Mustang Mk. Is were assigned the U. S. serial numbers 41-038 and 41-039. These two airplanes were sent to Wright Field, Ohio, for test and evaluation. The first, which was powered by the same Allison engine that had been installed in the NA-73X, first flew on May 20, 1941, but it did not arrive in Dayton until August 24.

While flying at Wright Field, Ohio, the second XP-51 received additional markings including the Wright arrowhead on the aft fuselage and the last four digits of its serial number on its nose and tail. A blue vertical band and red and white stripes had been added to the rudder. By this time, the British armament had been removed. (NMUSAF)

The second of the two XP-51s was photographed at NACA Langley Field, Virginia, on December 29, 1941. It remained in a natural metal finish at that time. (G. Balzer Collection)

The first XP-51, S/N 41-038, was painted in the standard Olive Drab over Neutral Gray scheme when it was photographed at NACA Langley Field on September 4, 1943. Note the instrumentation probe that has been added to the leading edge of the right wing. (G. Balzer Collection)

The second XP-51 did not arrive until December 16. By then, following the Japanese attack on Pearl Harbor, the chaos of mobilization was everywhere. There was still a lack of funds and personnel, and the entire country was in the process of changing over from a peacetime to a wartime footing. Priorities had to be established, and the top consideration had to be given to those fighters already rolling off the production lines. Accordingly, the evaluation of the new XP-51s could not begin immediately. When flight tests did begin, their performance and capabilities were already known, as demonstrated by the British Mustang Mk. Is. Compared to the P-40, which was then considered the best single-engine fighter in the U. S. Army Air Force's inventory, the XP-51 was superior in almost every performance criterion.

The XP-51s were essentially early Mustang Mk. I airframes with nose gun fairings. They were fitted with American radios such as the SCR-283 radio set. The control column was the U. S. style with the straight hand grip at the top, and an American compass was installed. The U. S. Army was not happy with the mixed battery of guns chosen by the British, so one XP-51 was sent to Eglin Field, Florida, for gun tests. Four 20mm cannons were selected for what would become the first U. S. production variant of the Mustang. Both XP-51s later were transferred to NACA following the end of the Eglin trials where they had long careers as aerodynamic test vehicles at Langley Field, Virginia. The first XP-51, 41-038, was restored to flying condition and today resides at the Experimental Aircraft Association Museum in Oshkosh, Wisconsin.

P-51-NA, F-6A, & MUSTANG Mk. IA

A Mustang Mk. IA, destined for service with the RAF, still has its U. S. national insignia while being flight tested before delivery. Note the dark residue on the wings from firing the four 20mm cannons. Like the Mustang Mk. Is, the Mk. IAs were originally delivered in the British brown and green camouflage scheme. (NAA via Piet)

On July 7, 1941, the Army placed an order with North American for 150 P-51-NAs. No suffix letter was placed after the P-51 designation, and it held the manufacturer's designation of NA-91. The order, while conservative in size, was made even though the two XP-51s had not yet arrived at Wright Field. This is clear evidence that the United States already recognized the significant potential of the design and was ready to commit to it as much as the available, but very limited funds, would permit.

Out of the 150 P-51-NAs ordered, S/N 41-37426, was bailed to the Navy for evaluation. More importantly, two were held back for testing with the Merlin engine. It was already

Fresh off the production lines, USAAF P-51-NAs and British Mustang Mk. IAs share the ramp at North American's plant. The four 20mm cannons were not installed until after the aircraft came off the production lines. The P-51s are painted in the Olive Drab over Neutral Gray scheme, while the Mustang Mk. IAs are in the British brown and green camouflage with the original fin flash, consisting of red, white, and blue segments of equal size. The engine exhaust ports were changed to the flattened "fishtail" style that is clearly visible on the aircraft at right. The hinged radiator scoop is also visible in the closed position. Note the colors of the landing gear struts and doors. (NAA via Piet)

A P-51-NA assigned to a training unit rests on a snow-covered field between flights. The radiator scoop is in the lowered position, and the exhaust vent is also open aft of it. As with all Allison-powered Mustangs, the inner main gear doors usually remained in the locked-up position when the aircraft was on the ground. (NMUSAF)

well known that these early Mustangs, with the Allison engine and its turbocharger installed, were excellent low-level fighters. However, they lacked excellent performance at higher altitudes. The fact that the Army retained two P-51-NAs for Merlin engine tests is unmistakable proof that it was already planning to develop high-altitude versions of the fighter as soon as possible. Further, the claims that the U. S. was not interested in the Mustang, and that its testing and evaluation were mishandled, can't be substantiated by documented facts.

The P-51-NA retained nearly all of the features of the British Mustang Mk. I. These included the single landing/taxi light on the leading edge of each wing and the hinged air inlet scoop. A major change involved replacing the mixed RAF battery of wing-mounted .50 and .303-caliber machine guns with four 20mm cannons mounted in pairs in the wings, and the nose guns were deleted. Each 20mm cannon was supplied with 125 rounds of ammunition, and this provided a firing time of 12.5 seconds. The internal structure of the wings was also strengthened, in part to accommodate the new cannons.

These aircraft had either the SCR-274 or -522 command radios. The radio sets were mounted on the aft cockpit deck behind the pilot's headrest and the rollover structure. A mast behind the cockpit connected a long antenna aerial to the cap of the vertical stabilizer, and depending on the radio fit, a second, short antenna extended from an insulator just aft of the mast to the top of the fuselage just behind the canopy. The

exhaust ports for the engine were changed from a circular to a flattened "fishtail" cross section that were more aerodynamic.

Fifty-five P-51-NAs were destined to serve in the newly renamed U. S. Army Air Forces. Ninety-three examples of this production run went to the British who dubbed them Mustang Mk. IAs. Fifty-seven P-51-NAs were converted into reconnaissance aircraft designated F-6As. Typically, they carried two K-24 cameras. One provided oblique views and was mounted behind the pilot's head just as in the British configuration. However, the K-24 was larger than the British F.24 camera. A bulged aft canopy fairing was installed to accommodate the oblique camera. The vertical camera was located in the lower rear fuselage behind the radiator exhaust but forward of the tail landing gear. The camera frame position could be remotely controlled by the pilot to move between vertical and rear-facing oblique angles. Camera controls were added to the cockpit.

The first combat use of any USAAF Mustang variant was during April 1943. The mission was flown in North Africa by the 154th Observation Squadron using a camera-equipped F-6A.

Serial Numbers for the P-51s that were delivered to the U. S. Army Air Forces were 41-37320 through 41-37469, and these include the ones converted to photo-reconnaissance F-6As. British Mustang Mk. IAs had RAF serials FD418 through FD567. However, it should be noted that the fifty-five P-51-NAs that went to the USAAF originally had British serial numbers within this range.

P-51-NA & MUSTANG Mk. IA

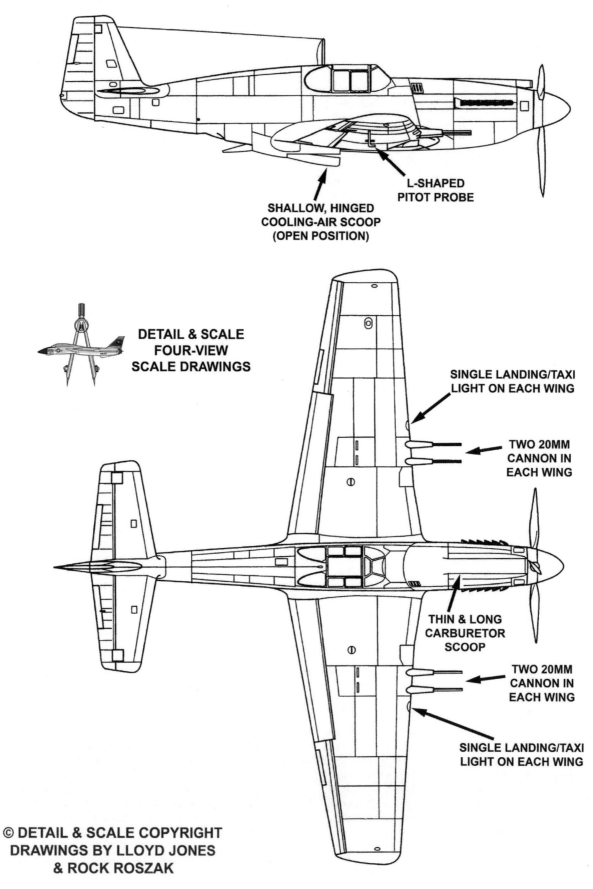

L-SHAPED
PITOT PROBE

SHALLOW, HINGED
COOLING-AIR SCOOP
(OPEN POSITION)

DETAIL & SCALE
FOUR-VIEW
SCALE DRAWINGS

SINGLE LANDING/TAXI
LIGHT ON EACH WING

TWO 20MM
CANNON IN
EACH WING

THIN & LONG
CARBURETOR
SCOOP

TWO 20MM
CANNON IN
EACH WING

SINGLE LANDING/TAXI
LIGHT ON EACH WING

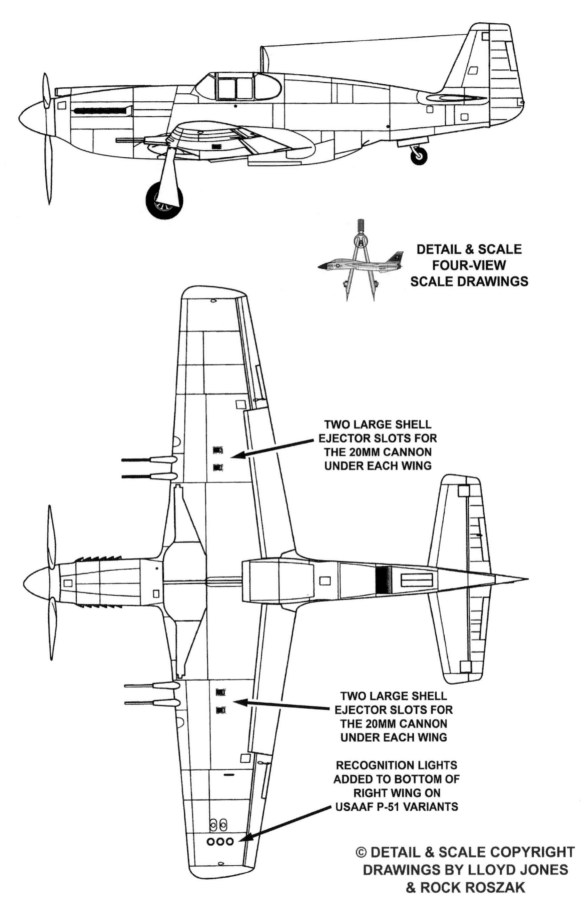

DETAIL & SCALE
FOUR-VIEW
SCALE DRAWINGS

TWO LARGE SHELL
EJECTOR SLOTS FOR
THE 20MM CANNON
UNDER EACH WING

TWO LARGE SHELL
EJECTOR SLOTS FOR
THE 20MM CANNON
UNDER EACH WING

RECOGNITION LIGHTS
ADDED TO BOTTOM OF
RIGHT WING ON
USAAF P-51 VARIANTS

S/N 41-37321 was the second P-51-NA built. It was delivered without the 20mm cannons installed, and it was used by North American Aviation as a test aircraft. Note the NAA logo on the vertical tail. It also retained the original engine exhaust ports with the circular cross section. (G. Balzer Collection)

Above: Perhaps the most unusual paint scheme to grace a Mustang was a "dazzle scheme" tested on a P-51-NA at Wright Field. The aim was to confuse an observer as to an airplane's direction, shape, and size long enough to gain an advantage over their opponent. The concept was inspired by the splinter schemes used on ships at sea. It was not adopted for operational use. (G. Balzer Collection).

Right: The P-51-NA and Mustang Mk. IA retained the hinged radiator scoop under the fuselage, along with the original design for the movable vent aft of it. (NMUSAF)

Ninety-three P-51-NA aircraft were acquired by Great Britain and were designated as the Mustang Mk. IA. They were identical to the American version, and the British used them for armed reconnaissance missions, fitted with cameras in the same manner as the Mustang Mk. Is. This Mk. IA was repainted in the gray and green camouflage scheme, and it has the later style fin flash with the narrow white segment at the center. (Piet Collection)

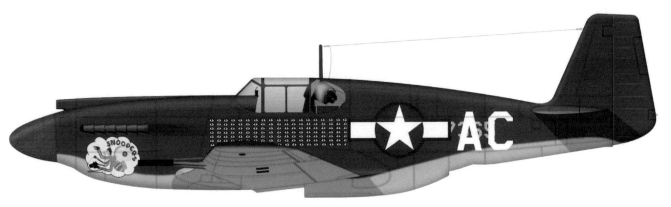

The "Snoopers" of the 111th Tactical Reconnaissance Squadron received F-6As in March 1943 and flew missions in Tunisia during the North African Campaign. They later moved on to Sicily providing valuable photograph reconnaissance to Generals Patton and Montgomery. Once Sicily was secured, the squadron flew countless missions in Italy. This profile of one of their F-6As displays 133 mission markings on its fuselage. (Roszak)

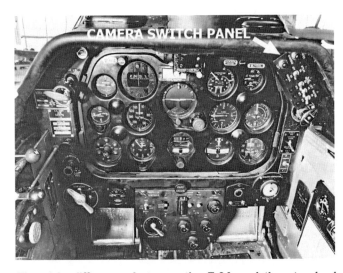

The only difference between the F-6A and the standard P-51 instrument panel was the addition of the Camera Switch Panel in the upper right corner of the panel. (G. Balzer Collection)

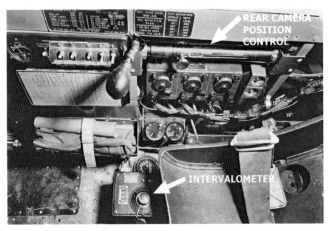

Additional items in the F-6A cockpit included an intervalometer located on the floor just forward of the seat on the right side. A tube-shaped device with a sliding handle, located high on the right side of the cockpit, allowed the pilot to switch the rear camera between the vertical and rear oblique positions in flight. (G. Balzer Collection)

Above and right: The British used an F.24 camera in its Mustang Mk. Is and Mk. IAs, and it fit inside the cockpit aft of the pilot's seat. The camera was small enough that it was not necessary for the RAF to redesign the rear window of their Mustangs. They only had to have a circular cutout in the window through which the camera could take photographs. This arrangement with the smaller camera was used on some USAAF F-6As and F-6Bs. However, the K-24 camera used by the USAAF in some F-6As (and subsequent F-6Bs) was larger than the British F.24 camera, and it required a blistered rear window to mount the camera. These two photographs show the K-24 camera and its blistered window on an F-6A at Wright Field. (Both, G. Balzer Collection)

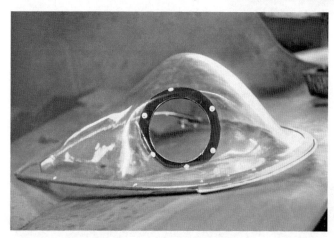

The blistered camera window had a framed circular opening through which the larger K-24 camera took photographs. There was no glass in the opening, so as not to cause distortion in the photos and to eliminate any potential fogging that might occur. (G. Balzer Collection)

Without the window installed, details of the camera and the structure on which it was mounted are visible in this photograph. (G. Balzer Collection)

The F-6A and F-6B had a rear camera installation in the aft fuselage between the vent for the radiator and the tail landing gear. In the photo at left, the camera is mounted in the vertical position. At right, the camera is mounted in the aft-looking oblique position. The pilot could switch the camera between these two positions while in flight. In each case, aft is to the right in the photographs. (Both, G. Balzer Collection)

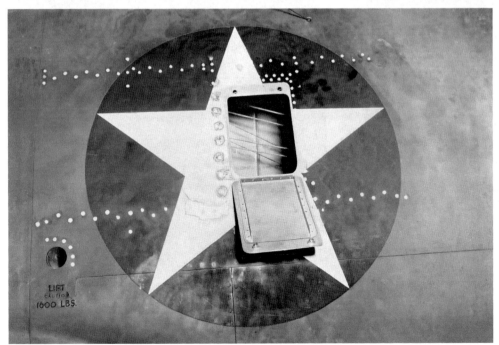

Center left: Taken from inside the aft fuselage, this photograph looks down at the rear camera installed in the vertical position. (G. Balzer Collection)

Center right: Taken from the same location as the photo at center left, the mount for the rear camera is shown in the vertical position but without the camera installed. (G. Balzer Collection)

Left: The film magazine for the aft camera could be loaded and unloaded through an access panel on the right side of the aft fuselage. (G. Balzer Collection)

Pilots assigned to a stateside training unit pose in front of one of their A-36As. This dive-bomber variant was the most numerous of all of the USAAF Allison-powered Mustangs. (Bell Collection)

As the Pursuit Projects Officer at Wright Field, Lt. Benjamin Kelsey kept the American side of the Mustang program alive by coming up with the idea of developing it as a dive bomber. Even though dive bombers were never very popular with the USAAF, it was the excuse Kelsey needed to increase the U. S. involvement in the program. Lt. Kelsey's ingenuity and foresight led to procurement of 500 A-36As beginning in 1942. This would be the largest order of Allison-powered Mustangs by the United States. Although one A-36 (RAF serial number EW998) was shipped to England for evaluation, the British did not place an order for this variant.

North American model NA-97 was formally designated by the USAAF as the A-36A. However, it was most often simply called the A-36, since no other variants were produced. North American initially chose the name "Apache" for the aircraft ordered by the United States, but "Mustang" was already well established and remained the official USAAF name for the A-36. Regardless, the A-36 was commonly referred to as the

Apache, although it was unofficial as far as the USAAF was concerned. An attempt to call the A-36 the "Invader" by units in Sicily and Italy also failed. That name was later bestowed on the Douglas A-26.

For use as a dive bomber, the A-36A differed considerably from all previous Mustang variants. It was envisioned that the dive bomber would operate primarily at altitudes below 12,000 feet. Accordingly, the V-1710-87 version of the Allison engine, optimized for low-level performance, was chosen, and it was fitted with a single-stage, single-speed supercharger. Although not dictated by the change in role from fighter to dive bomber, the radiator intake scoop was changed from the previous hinged design to a fixed inlet. An air filter was placed inside the carburetor scoop, and this resulted in a wider inlet than those of previous variants. The propeller blades were made of aluminum, rather than steel.

Dive brakes were added to the top and bottom of each wing. This prevented the installation of the L-shaped pitot

Red, yellow, and blue spinners adorn A-36s of a stateside training unit. These training units often had large aircraft numbers painted on each side of their forward fuselage beneath the exhaust ports. (Bell Collection)

Field conditions in Sicily and Italy were certainly not as good as those for stateside training units that enjoyed paved parking aprons and runways. Instead, the field conditions were often quite muddy, as seen in this photograph taken in Italy. Note the two kill markings on the nose of this A-36. (G. Balzer Collection)

probe which had been mounted under the right wing on the fighter versions. Instead, a pitot boom was installed on the leading edge of the right wing near the tip. The overdue addition of a relief tube in the cockpit was well received among aircrews.

Underwing bomb racks, each of which could carry up to a 500-pound bomb, were mounted just outboard of the landing gear. During a dive-bombing attack, both bombs were released simultaneously. These racks could also be used to carry either external 75-gallon fuel tanks or 125-gallon ferry tanks. The A-36 had two landing/taxi lights; however, these lights were not mounted as single units on each wing as had been the case with the earlier Mustang Mk. I and the P-51-NA/Mustang Mk. IA. Instead, both lights were located together in one large mounting on the leading edge of the left wing. A flare compartment was added behind the cockpit.

To give the A-36 enhanced firepower with which to strafe, the USAAF opted for six .50-caliber machine guns. Four of these were in the wings and replaced the P-51-NA's 20mm cannons. The other two were chin mounted as they had been on the Mustang Mk. I. However, the small fairings found on the earlier British variant were not used on the A-36. Up to 350 rounds could be loaded for each outboard machine gun in the wings, while 250 rounds could be loaded for each inboard weapon. Each machine gun in the nose was supplied with 200 rounds of ammunition. The standard practice was to load 200 rounds for each of the six guns, although one report states that a maximum of 1,100 rounds could be loaded. It

should also be noted that the two cowl-mounted guns were sometimes removed in the field, because they made the aircraft nose heavy. Since the aircraft was already nose heavy with the guns installed, removing them did not require the use of ballast to compensate for the reduction in forward weight. When the nose guns were removed, the maximum load of ammunition could be used for the four wing guns. The machine guns were aimed through an optical reflector type gunsight, and a ring and bead backup sight was usually present. The N-1 gun camera was mounted between the nose guns.

The radio sets were carried over from the P-51-NA, and the A-36's IFF gear could vary between the SCR-515, SCR-535, and SCR-695 systems. With the SCR-522, a thick, insulated antenna mast replaced the earlier thin mast design. Depending on the IFF radios installed, A-36s could be fitted with a pair of dipole antennas under each wing just outboard of the wing roots (SCR-515), either one or two IFF antenna aerials strung between the fuselage and the horizontal stabilizers (SCR-535), or a single dipole antenna under the right outer wing (SCR-695).

Although it fought at low altitudes in the face of intense anti-aircraft fire, only 177 A-36s were lost in combat to enemy action. These losses came while flying more than 23,300 combat sorties. This is an average of only one aircraft lost every 130 missions. This testifies not only to the design of the aircraft but to the skill and talent of their pilots.

USAAF serial numbers for the A-36A were 42-83663 through 42-84162.

One A-36 was delivered to the Royal Air Force for testing; however, the British opted not to place an order for the dive-bomber variant of the Mustang. (G. Balzer Collection)

A-36

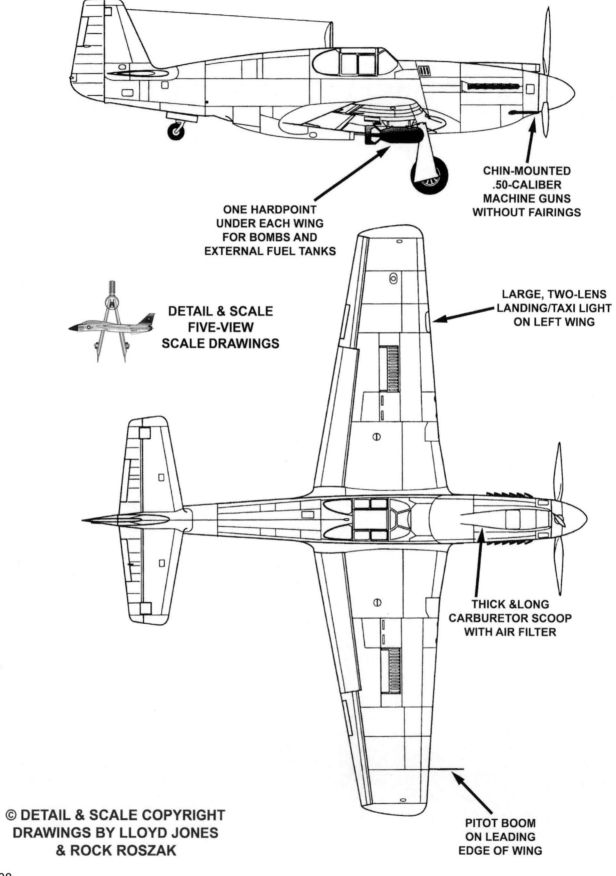

ONE HARDPOINT
UNDER EACH WING
FOR BOMBS AND
EXTERNAL FUEL TANKS

CHIN-MOUNTED
.50-CALIBER
MACHINE GUNS
WITHOUT FAIRINGS

**DETAIL & SCALE
FIVE-VIEW
SCALE DRAWINGS**

LARGE, TWO-LENS
LANDING/TAXI LIGHT
ON LEFT WING

THICK &LONG
CARBURETOR SCOOP
WITH AIR FILTER

PITOT BOOM
ON LEADING
EDGE OF WING

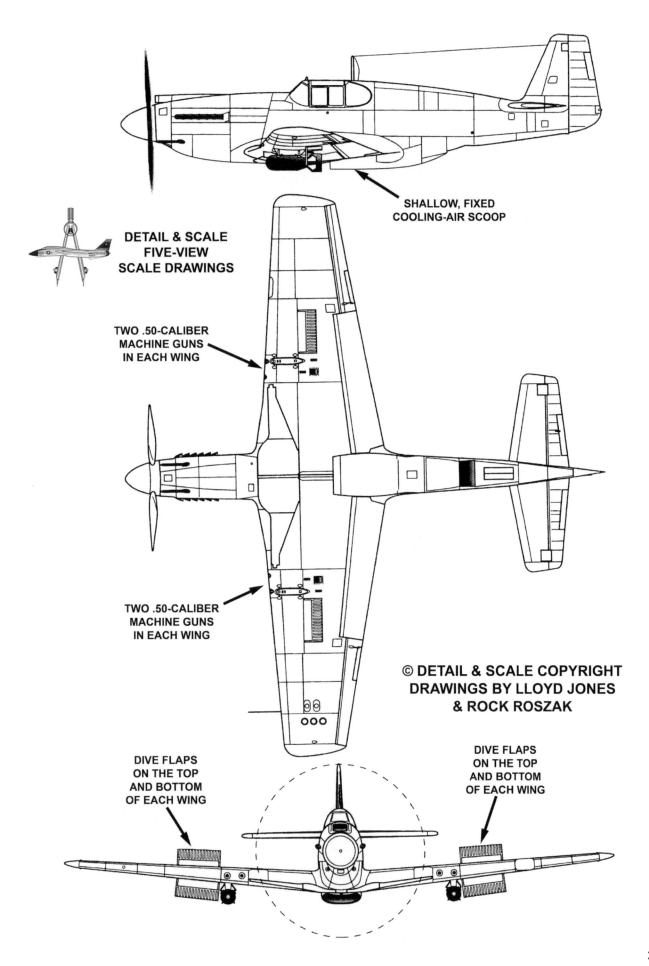

SHALLOW, FIXED
COOLING-AIR SCOOP

DETAIL & SCALE
FIVE-VIEW
SCALE DRAWINGS

TWO .50-CALIBER
MACHINE GUNS
IN EACH WING

TWO .50-CALIBER
MACHINE GUNS
IN EACH WING

© DETAIL & SCALE COPYRIGHT
DRAWINGS BY LLOYD JONES
& ROCK ROSZAK

DIVE FLAPS
ON THE TOP
AND BOTTOM
OF EACH WING

DIVE FLAPS
ON THE TOP
AND BOTTOM
OF EACH WING

39

The color photographs on this page and the next illustrate the A-36, S/N 42-83901, flown by Major John R. Crowder Jr. when he commanded the 524th Fighter Bomber Squadron of the 27th Fighter Bomber Group. They provide an interesting study of the details of the aircraft and the evolution of its markings during the time it was in service. In this first photo, its original markings are revealed. These include the national insignia used in early 1943 with the yellow surround that was added for Operation Torch in Africa. The A*A codes are on the fuselage with the last six digits of the serial number in yellow farther aft. (Crowder via Piet)

Right: Major Crowder poses in the cockpit of his A-36. This photograph provides a good look at some of the cockpit details, including the small window on the left side of the windscreen and the gunsight above the instrument panel. Note the cord that keeps the top part of the canopy from opening too far. The unusual antenna mast found on many A-36s is also visible. (Crowder via Piet)

Below: Additional details of the A-36 are revealed in this photo of Major Crowder and his crew chief, S/SGT E. A. Radabaugh. Noteworthy are the colors of the landing gear. A-36s operating in North Africa, and later in Sicily and Italy, usually had yellow bands on the wings as an identification feature to distinguish them from German and Italian aircraft. (Crowder via Piet)

The nose art on Major Crowder's A-36 included the name "Dorothy Helen," mission makings in the form of yellow bombs, and the names of the pilot, crew chief, and two other members of the ground crew. Note that the machine guns in the nose have been removed. This was often done in the field, because the guns and their ammunition made the A-36 a little nose heavy. Because the aircraft was nose heavy with the guns, removing them did not require the addition of ballast to compensate for the change in the center of balance. (Crowder via Piet)

The original markings on the left side of the aft fuselage are revealed in this photograph. They include the national insignia with the yellow surround, the A*A fuselage codes in white, and the last six digits of the serial number in yellow. P-51As and A-36s operating in the Mediterranean Theater often had yellow geometric markings on the aft fuselage and vertical tail. An example is on this A-36 above the serial number. Note the open dive brakes. (Crowder via Piet)

On June 29, 1943, the American national insignia was changed to one with white rectangles on either side of the blue disc with the white star, and a red outline surrounded the entire insignia. Major Crowder's A-36 was repainted with this style of insignia, and it necessitated moving the A*A codes to the vertical tail. The red surround was deleted by directive on September 17, 1943, but it would remain on many aircraft for some time after that date. This photo was taken at Gela, Sicily, after that change was made. All other markings remain unchanged. (Crowder via Piet)

These two photographs are of the same A-36 which was piloted by Robert L. Bryant. The crew chief was S/SGT Dan Perez. The photo at left was taken in Sicily, while the one at right was taken in Pastuem, Italy, in November 1943. Again, note that the nose guns have been removed from this A-36. (Both, NMUSAF)

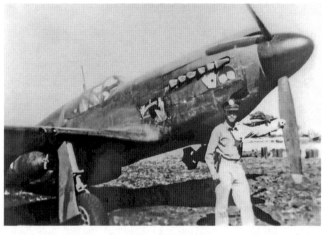

"Manaleene" was flown by Mark A. "Doe" Savage. This A-36 was assigned to the 533rd Fighter Bomber Squadron of the 27th Fighter Bomber Group. The photograph was taken at Salerno, Italy, in 1943. (NMUSAF)

"DOT" was another A-36 assigned to the 27th Fighter Bomber Group. Note the open dive brakes as the pilot runs up the engine prior to taxiing out for takeoff. A ground crewman sits on the wing to help guide the pilot as he taxis. (NMUSAF)

"Margie H." was an A-36 from the 533rd Fighter Bomber Squadron of the 27th Fighter Bomber Group. The original "Margie H." is pictured with its pilot and ground crew in the photo at left. The restored A-36, on display at the National Museum of the U. S. Air Force, is marked to represent this aircraft; however, it is not the original "Margie H." as has been reported elsewhere. (Both, NMUSAF)

A-36 COCKPIT DETAILS

The items on the instrument panel of an A-36 are identified in this photograph that was taken from the flight manual. Keys for the numbered items are provided at right. (NMUSAF)

1. Cockpit Fluorescent Light
2. Windshield Defroster Control
3. Gun Sight
4. Ring and Bead Gun Sight (Stowed Position)
5. Windshield De-icer Spray Control
6. Cockpit florescent Light
7. LH Gun Charging Handle
8. Magnetic Compass
9. Clock
10. Suction Gage
11. Manifold Pressure Gage
12. RH Gun Charging Handle
13. Throttle
14. Accelerometer
15. Remote Contactor
16. Altimeter
17. Turn Indicator
18. Flight Indicator
19. Tachometer
20. Oxygen Flow Indicator
21. Enclosure Emergency Release Handle
22. Propeller Constant Speed Control
23. Landing Gear Emergency Down Control
24. Landing Gear Electrical Position Indicator
25. Air Speed Indicator
26. Turn and Bank Indicator
27. Rate-of-Climb Indicator
28. Coolant Temperature Indicator
29. Oil Temperature and Fuel and Oil Gage
30. Oxygen Flow Regulator
31. Carburetor Air Control
32. Contactor Heater Switch
33. Parking Brake Control Handle
34. Automatic Flare Discharger Control
35. Gun and Camera Safety Switch

36. Gun Heater Switch
37. Bomb Nose-Arming Switch
38. Bomb Tail-Arming Switch
39. Bomb Safety Switch
40. Propeller Selector Switch
41. Propeller Circuit Breaker Button
42. Oil Dilution Switch
43. Compass Light Switch and Rheostat Control
44. Cockpit Lights Switch and Rheostat Control
45. Engine Primer
46. Hydraulic Pressure Gage
47. Instrument Static Selector Valve
48. Bomb Control Handle
49. Ignition Switch
50. Starter Switch
51. Fuel Booster Pump Switch
52. Gun Sight Switch and Rheostat Control
53. LH Florescent Light control
54. Landing Gear Control Handle
55. Leg-Length Adjustment Pins
56. Main Fuel System Selector Valve
57. Auxiliary Fuel System Selector Valve
58. Cockpit Cold-Air Ventilation Valve
59. Surface Control Lock
60. Hydraulic Hand Pump

The left side of the cockpit is shown at left, while at right is a photograph of the right side. Keys for these two photographs are provided below, except that numbers less than 61 are the same as the keys included in the list above. (Both, NMUSAF)

61. Recognition Light Keying Switch
62. Sliding Window Control
63. Spare Lamp Compartment
64. Pitot Heater Switch
65. White Recognition Light Switch
66. Red Recognition Light Switch
67. Green Recognition Light Switch
68. Amber Recognition Light Switch
69. Wing Navigation Light Switch
70. Tail Navigation Light Switch
71. RH Florescent Light Control
72. Landing Light Switch
73. Generator Disconnect Switch
74. Ammeter
75. Transmitter Key
76. Earphone Jack
77. Microphone Jack

78. Cockpit Light
79. Transmitter Light Selector Switch
80. Transmitter Power Toggle Switch
81. Transmitter Selector Switch
82. Jack Selector Switch, 3-6 MC
83. Receiver Signal Selector Switch, 3-6 MC
84. Jack Selector Switch, 190-550 KC
85. Receiver Signal Selector Switch, 190-550 KC
86. Jack Selector Switch, 6-9.1 MC
87. Receiver Signal Selector Switch, 6-9.1 MC
88. Receiver Volume Control, 3-6 MC
89. Receiver Frequency Control, 3-6 MC
90. Receiver Volume Control, 190-550 KC
91. Receiver Frequency Control, 190-550 KC
92. Receiver Volume Control, 6-9.1 MC
93. Receiver Frequency Control, 6-9.1 MC
94. Filter Switch Control

95. Right Fuel Tank Gage
96. Microphone Press-To-Talk Switch
97. Mixture Control
98. Cockpit Light
99. Dive-Brake Control
100. Quadrant Friction Control
101. Flap Position Indicator
102. Radiator Air Scoop Position Indicator
103. Flap Control handle
104. Radiator Air Scoop Control Handle
105. Rudder Trim Tab Control
106. Aileron Trim Tab Control
107. Landing Gear Mechanical Position Indicator
108. Bomb Control Anti-Salvo Guard
109. Tail Wheel Lock Control
110. Elevator Trim Tab Control

A-36 DETAILS

Above: The A-36 had six .50-caliber machine guns, two of which were mounted in the nose beneath the engine. Note that the right barrel does not extend as far forward as the left barrel. Here, one mechanic works in the engine accessory compartment while another performs checks on the right side gun. (Bell Collection)

Right: With panels removed, details of the left side machine gun are revealed. The ammunition box is installed, but no rounds are in it. Up to 200 rounds could be loaded for each nose gun. This was the same installation as used on the Mustang Mk. I, except that the A-36 did not have the fairings around the gun barrels where they exited the nose. (NAA via Piet)

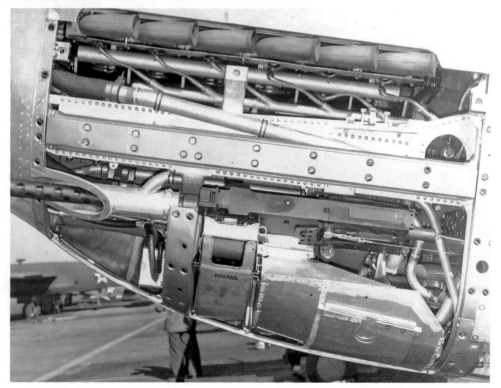

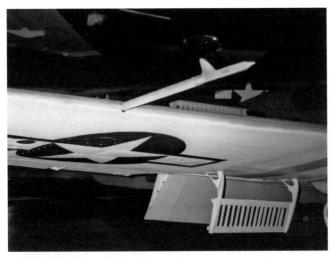

Because dive brakes were added to both upper and lower surfaces of the wings of the A-36, the L-shaped pitot probe that was located under the right wing of other Mustang variants could not be used on the dive bomber variant. Instead, a pitot boom was mounted on the leading edge of the right wing. (Kinzey)

Unlike the previous Mustang variants which had a single landing/taxi light in the leading edge of each wing, the A-36 had two lights located together in the leading edge of the left wing. This arrangement was unique to the A-36. (Kinzey)

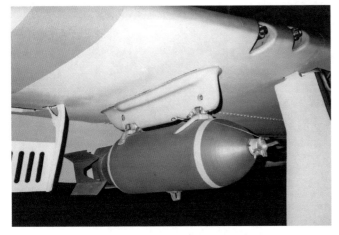

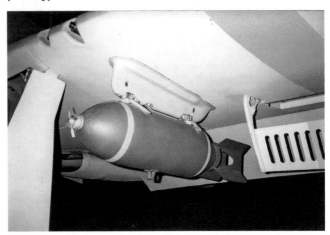

The A-36 was the first variant of the Mustang to have hardpoints and racks under the wings for carrying external stores. On the A-36, these were primarily used to carry bombs up to the 500-pound size, but 75-gallon and 125-gallon external fuel tanks could also be carried. These hardpoints with their racks remained standard on the subsequent P-51A and later on the Merlin-powered Mustang variants. (Both, Kinzey)

Armorers load bombs on A-36s of the 27th Fighter Bomber Group in Italy. In the photo at left, note that the fins of the loaded bombs are in the + position rather than the more common X position. (Both, G. Balzer Collection)

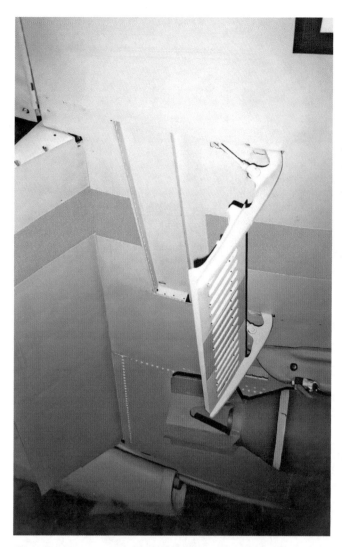

Dive bombers require dive brakes to perform their mission and to remain relatively slow and stable in steep dives. The A-36 had four dive brakes, one on the top and one on the bottom of each wing. The dive brake under the right wing swung forward to open. (Kinzey)

The dive brake on top of the right wing operated in the opposite direction. It swung aft to open. The reason for this difference was to provide room inside the wing for the mechanism that operated the two brakes. Note the well into which the brake fit when closed. (Kinzey)

Additional details, including the well, hinges, and actuation links for the speed brake beneath the right wing are revealed in these two photographs. (Both, Kinzey)

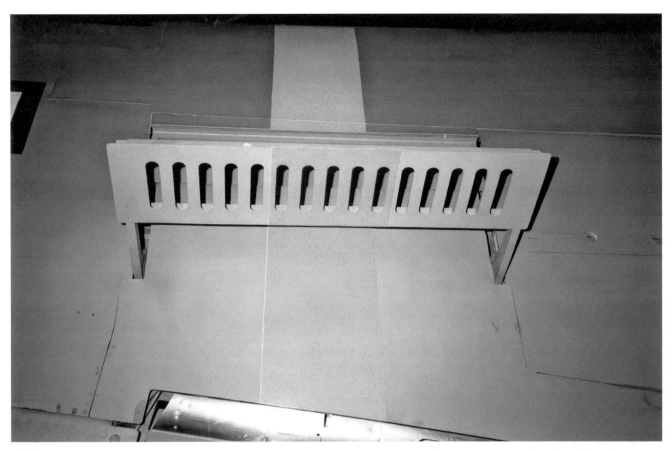

The speed brakes on the left wing were identical to those on the right wing. The brake on top of the wing opened aft, as illustrated here from behind the brake. (Kinzey)

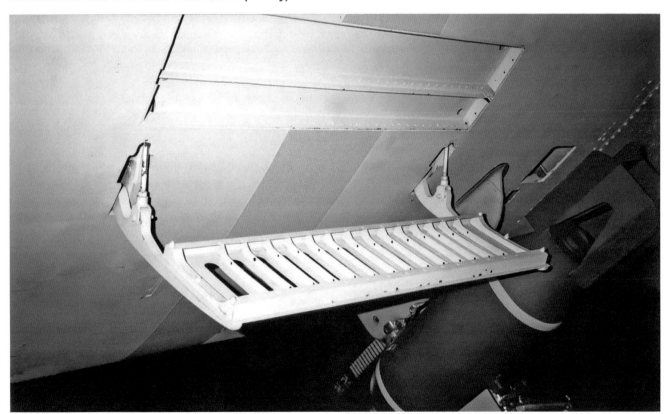

The lower speed brake on the bottom of the left wing opened forward. The speed brakes were located just outboard of the pylons that carried the bombs and external fuel tanks. (Kinzey)

P-51A, F-6B, & MUSTANG Mk. II

P-51As of the 1st Air Commando Group are lined up on a field in China. The 1st ACG used diagonal white stripes on the aft fuselage as a means of identifying their aircraft. Their Mustangs had polished natural metal spinners, and on some aircraft the wing tips and the fin cap on top of the vertical stabilizer were also shiny natural metal. (Piet Collection)

The baseline P-51A was essentially an A-36A without the dive-bombing equipment. It had the same air filter in the carburetor air scoop with the wider design. The same bomb racks were standard for carriage of up to 500-pound bombs or external fuel tanks. In some cases, other stores, like smoke generators, were also carried by P-51As.

The P-51A probably contained the largest collection of engineering and design changes of any new Mustang variant to that point. They were built across three production blocks: P-51A-1-NA, P-51A-5-NA, and P-51A-10-NA, and thirty-five were converted into F-6Bs. The camera gear and mounts were identical to that of the F-6A, illustrated previously in the P-51-NA section of this chapter. The -5 and -10 blocks each introduced additional improvements to the previous block.

A major goal was to make the aircraft as light as possible. Beginning with the P-51A-1-NA, fuselage longeron and stringer configurations were redesigned to be stronger and lighter. Even slightly lighter (thinner) gauge aluminum was used in various places. The gunsight was upgraded to the N-1 type and the canopy was revised to improve visibility. A few F-6Bs were modified with the Malcolm hood style canopy to improve visibility. The P-51A deleted the flare dispenser in the rear fuselage and introduced an M-8 flare gun that could be fired through a port on the left side of the cockpit. Early P-51As featured the same range of radio fits as the A-36A. Later, they were standardized to SCR-522 as the onboard radio paired with the SCR-695 IFF system.

To give the P-51A improved performance at higher altitudes, the Allison V-1710-81 engine was installed. It had an improved supercharger, but it still could not match the performance of the turbo-supercharger used with the V-1710 in the P-38 Lightning or the subsequent Rolls Royce/Packard Merlin engine.

The radiator system was unique. A U-shaped ethylene glycol radiator, only seen in the P-51A, was fitted around the standard cylindrical oil cooler unit. This made the radiator assembly wider but shorter, and the inlet and exit flap were also redesigned. The L-shaped pitot probe returned to the underside of the right wing, and it stayed there on all subsequent Mustangs. There was only one landing/taxi light mounted in the leading edge of the left wing instead of the dual unit found on the A-36A.

To make the aircraft lighter, the two chin-mounted guns were deleted, leaving the P-51A with only four .50-caliber machine guns in the wings. The standard ammunition load was 275 rounds per gun, but a maximum of 350 rounds could be squeezed into the forward ammunition boxes and 280 rounds loaded into the rear boxes. The gun camera was moved from the engine cowling to the inboard left leading edge of the wing. In some cases during operational use, P-51As were fitted with triple rocket tubes under the wings.

Originally, 1,200 P-51As were ordered, but this number was cut to 310 in December 1942. During the previous month, the first XP-51B had flown with the Merlin engine. P-51A

"Slick Chick" was S/N 43-6004, the second P-51A to come off the production line. It was delivered in a natural metal finish, and it served as a test aircraft at Wright Field, Ohio. Note the serial number lettered under the left wing. (NMUSAF)

production was accordingly truncated in favor of starting the manufacture of the P-51B and P-51C. Fifty P-51As were sent to the Royal Air Force where they received the designation Mustang Mk. II. Mustang Mk. IIs were fitted with cameras and used exclusively in the reconnaissance role. Consequently, they never flew operationally with bomb racks. They also carried American radio gear or their British equivalents. The underwing recognition lights were removed from the Mustang Mk. II.

The first unit to take the P-51A into combat was the 311th Fighter Bomber Group based in India. This group also flew the A-36A, and the use of two very similar aircraft simplified operations, maintenance, and logistics. Other units to operate the type were the 23rd Fighter Group and the 1st Air Commando Group.

The serial numbers for the three production blocks of P-51As were:

P-51A-1-NA	43-6003 through 43-6102
P-51A-5-NA	43-6103 through 43-6157
P-51A-10-NA	43-6158 through 43-6312

The British serial numbers for the Mustang Mk. IIs were:

FR890 through FR939

Although most P-51As served in the Olive Drab over Neutral Gray scheme, this Mustang is in natural metal. P-51A-10-NA, S/N 43-6178, was from the final production block for this variant. (Jones Collection)

P-51A, S/N 43-6008, was the sixth P-51A built, and it was used as a test aircraft for a water injection system for the Allison powerplant. (NAA via Piet)

49

P-51A & MUSTANG Mk. II

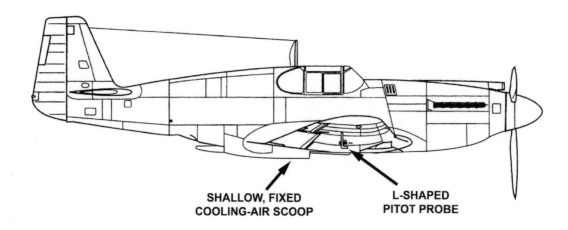

SHALLOW, FIXED
COOLING-AIR SCOOP

L-SHAPED
PITOT PROBE

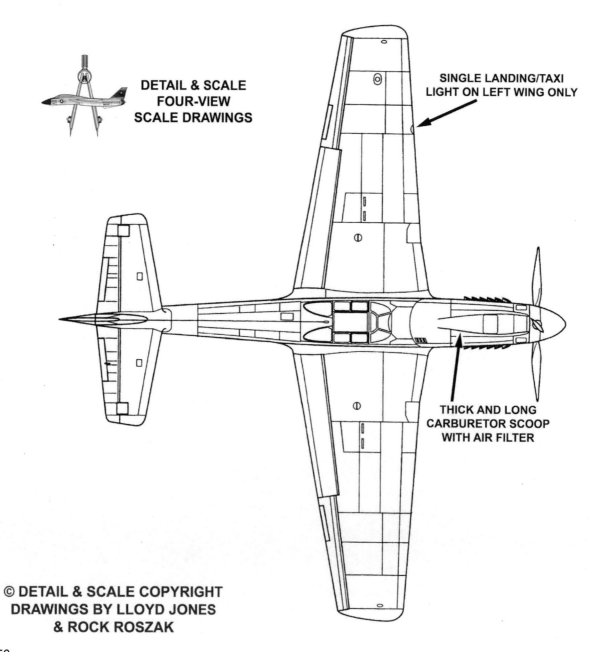

DETAIL & SCALE
FOUR-VIEW
SCALE DRAWINGS

SINGLE LANDING/TAXI
LIGHT ON LEFT WING ONLY

THICK AND LONG
CARBURETOR SCOOP
WITH AIR FILTER

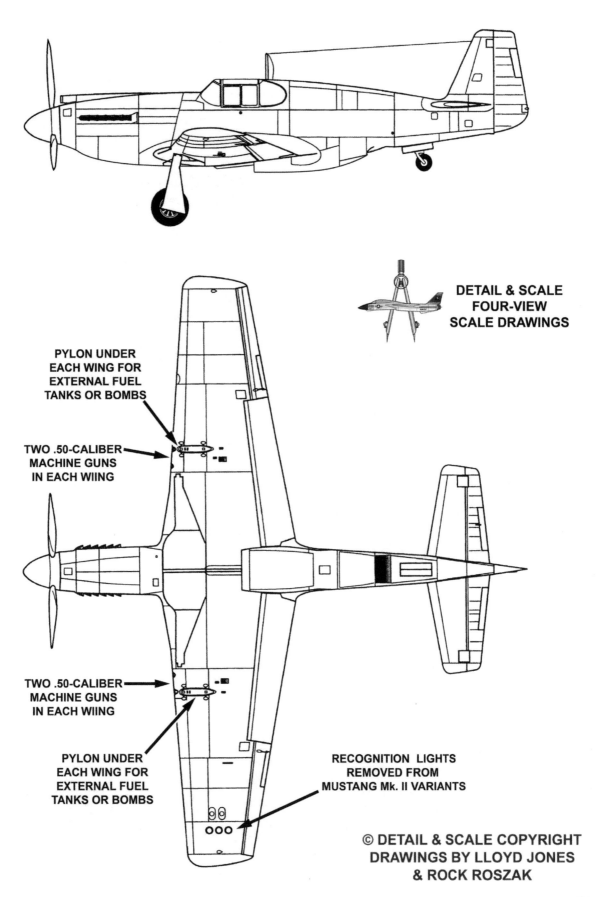

DETAIL & SCALE
FOUR-VIEW
SCALE DRAWINGS

PYLON UNDER
EACH WING FOR
EXTERNAL FUEL
TANKS OR BOMBS

TWO .50-CALIBER
MACHINE GUNS
IN EACH WIING

TWO .50-CALIBER
MACHINE GUNS
IN EACH WIING

PYLON UNDER
EACH WING FOR
EXTERNAL FUEL
TANKS OR BOMBS

RECOGNITION LIGHTS
REMOVED FROM
MUSTANG Mk. II VARIANTS

© DETAIL & SCALE COPYRIGHT
DRAWINGS BY LLOYD JONES
& ROCK ROSZAK

The very first P-51A produced was one of two that were flown to Ladd Field, Alaska, for testing with skis in place of the standard landing gear. Even with the skis in place, the landing gear could be fully retracted. Note the recontoured fuselage just forward of the wing root where the right ski fit when retracted. (NMUSAF)

With few exceptions, P-51As were delivered in the USAAF's Olive Drab over Neutral Gray paint scheme. Initially, the standard national insignia for late 1942 and early 1943, as seen here, was on a few early production P-51As. This consisted simply of an Insignia White star inside an Insignia Blue disc. In late June 1943, this was replaced with the national insignia that included the rectangles on the sides, and the entire insignia had a red surround. However, the red surround was short lived and was officially deleted by September 17 of that year. The last five digits of the serial number were stenciled in yellow numerals that were ten inches high. Note the dipole antenna mounted in the star area under the right wing. (G. Balzer Collection)

To increase the firepower of the P-51A in the ground attack role, triple-tube rocket launchers were tested on this Mustang, and also on an A-36A, at Eglin Field, Florida. Although these rocket tubes are known to have been used in combat on P-51As, particularly in the CBI theater, it appears that such use must have been relatively limited, because very few, if any, photographs of P-51As and A-36As in the field show the rocket tubes in place under the wings. (G. Balzer Collection)

Three P-51As fly together with smoke generators mounted under the wings. Compared to bombs and external fuel tanks, smoke generators were another seldom used external store for this early Mustang variant. Note that these P-51As have the later style national insignias without the red surround. (NAA via Piet)

Right: Captain J. J. England sits in the cockpit of his P-51A named "Jackie" as he chats with his crew chief. Captain England commanded the 530th Fighter Bomber Squadron of the 311th Fighter Bomber Group. A profile of this aircraft appears on the last page of this section. (Piet Collection)

Below: While the majority of the missions flown by P-51As were in the ground attack role, they also flew escort missions for bomber aircraft. Here a P-51A flies in formation with a B-24. Note that both aircraft have the national insignia with the red surround. (Piet Collection)

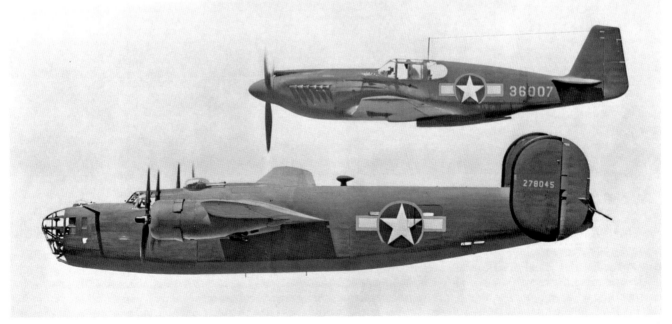

The best known unit to fly the P-51A was the 1st Air Commando Group in the China-Burma-India Theater. It consisted of a squadron of thirty P-51As, a squadron of twelve B-25H Mitchells, and squadrons of transports, utility aircraft, and other miscellaneous types. Its aircraft carried distinctive diagonal white stripes on the aft fuselage, and the stripes on the tail of this P-51A indicate a section leader. This particular P-51A has the shiny natural metal on the forward section of the spinner, but it does not have the natural metal wing tips or tip of the vertical stabilizer found on some 1st ACG P-51As. (Piet Collection)

Major Robert T. Smith commanded the squadron of B-25H Mitchell medium bombers in the 1st ACG; however, he often flew P-51As. His Mustangs were named "Barbie," and he is shown with the first of these in this photo. In this photograph and the one above, note the unusual arrangement of the wire antennas. P-51As assigned to the 1st ACG also had the loop antenna mounted on the spine of the fuselage. This was also common on other fighter type aircraft in the CBI theater. Note the natural metal color of the inside of the outer gear door on the right landing gear. (Piet Collection)

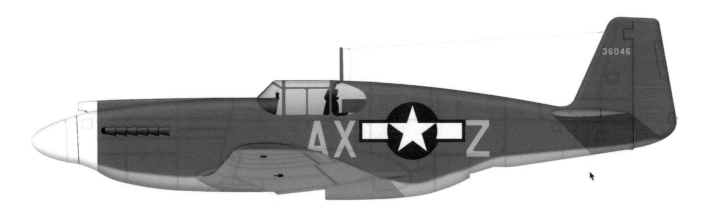

P-51A, S/N 43-6046, served with the 107th Tactical Reconnaissance Squadron. With the three-letter codes and later style national insignia on the fuselage, the last five digits of the serial number were moved to the vertical tail. (Roszak)

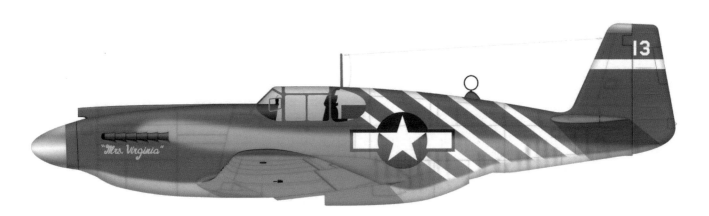

"Mrs. Virginia" was one of the better-known P-51As assigned to the 1st Air Commando Group. It had the polished natural metal spinner, and the fin cap at the top of the vertical stabilizer was also natural metal. (Roszak)

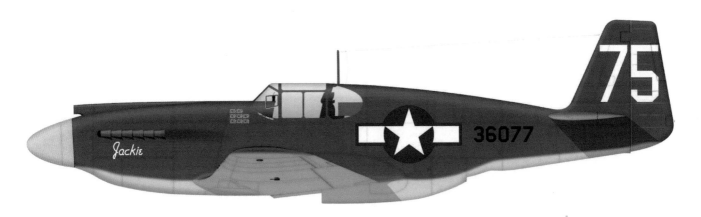

"Jackie" was the personal mount of Captain J. J. England who commanded the 530th Fighter Bomber Squadron of the 311th Fighter Bomber Group. Note that the serial number was stenciled in black on this aircraft. Major England claimed eight Japanese aircraft destroyed. (Roszak)

ALLISON-ENGINED MUSTANG DETAILS
COCKPIT DETAILS

A reflector gunsight was mounted at the center of the coaming above the instrument panel. To its right was a backup metal ring and bead sight. Most Allison-engined Mustangs had their rear-view mirror inside the cockpit, mounted at the top of the framework for the windscreen. Note the red landing gear warning light to the left. (Kinzey)

This full view provides a good look at the layout and details of the instrument panel in a P-51A. The cockpit was painted in Chromate Green primer, while the instrument panel was flat black. (Kinzey)

Left: Additional details of the instrument panel and the top of the control column are visible in this photograph taken from the right side. With relatively few detail differences, the cockpits in the other USAAF Allison-powered Mustang variants, except the A-36A, had a very similar appearance with regard to layout and colors. (Kinzey)

Bottom left: The floor in the cockpits of the Allison-engine Mustangs was simply the metal structure that formed the top of the curved center wing section. In this view, the silver rudder pedals are also visible. (Kinzey)

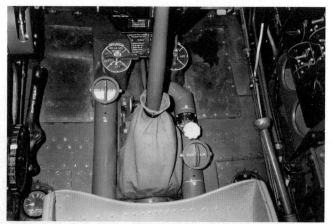

This closeup provides a good look at the details on the floor of the cockpit. These include both hot and cold air vents, fuel selector switches, and gauges. The black landing gear lever is to the left, and the emergency hydraulic hand pump is to the right. Note also the canvas boot around the base of the control column. (Kinzey)

Details on the left side of the cockpit include the engine and propeller controls, the red external stores release handle, and trim tab controls. The black landing gear lever is again visible at the base of the side wall. Farther aft, the small black handle on the black base is the Radiator Air Scoop Control Handle, and the lever with the yellow knob is the Flap Control Lever. The item in the top left corner is the port through which the flare gun could be fired. (Kinzey)

Controls for electrical equipment, including the radios, lights, and cockpit heating were on the right side of the cockpit. The radio equipment changed from one aircraft to the next, depending on where it was operating and other factors. The connection for the pilot's oxygen hose was forward on the right side, and the red handle above it released the canopy in an emergency. A wooden storage box for aircraft flight records and maps was aft on the right side. (Kinzey)

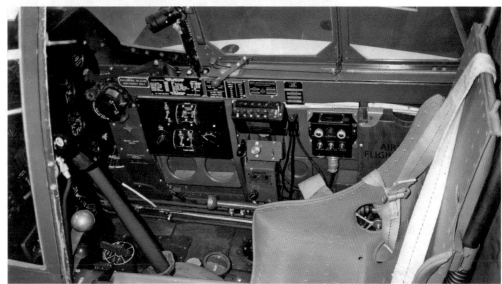

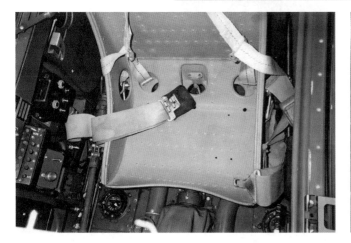

The Schick-Johnson bucket seat was attached to an armor plate that provided protection for the pilot. The seat could be moved up or down to position the pilot at the best height to provide a good view forward and to the sides of the aircraft. Visibility to the rear was very poor with the standard framed canopy. In this restored P-51A, the seat is painted Zinc Chromate Yellow primer, but vintage color photos indicate that the seats were usually the same Chromate Green primer, or a very similar color, like the rest of the cockpit. (Both, Kinzey)

WINDSCREEN & CANOPY DETAILS

Above: This photograph of two Women's Airforce Ferry Service Pilots (WASP) checking out the cockpit of a P-51A provides an excellent look at the original standard framed windscreen and canopy used on Mustangs. Many, but certainly not all, of these early Mustangs had a small framed window on the left side of the windscreen as seen here. The left side of the canopy hinged downward, and the top section hinged open to the right to provide access to the cockpit from the left side of the aircraft. (Bell Collection)

Right: Another vintage color photograph provides a good look at the left side of the standard canopy with the side and top panels open. The rear windows on these early Mustangs did not have the added attachment points seen on the later P-51B and P-51C Mustangs. Again, this P-51A has the small window on the left side of the windscreen. (Bell Collection)

58

Left and above: The windscreen had four framed sections. The front center panel was made of thick bullet-proof glass, and it was flanked by two side windows. As illustrated on the previous page, some early Mustangs, had a small framed window in the left side section of the windscreen, but others, as shown here, did not have that feature. Above these three sections was a small overhead section. (Both, Kinzey)

Details of the right side of windscreen and canopy enclosure in the closed position are illustrated in these two photographs. The right side of the canopy was fixed, and the top center section was hinged along its upper edge. This design meant that entrance to and egress from the cockpit could only be accomplished from the left side. Note also the triangular sections at the top and bottom of the leading edge of the framework for the rear window. (Both, Kinzey)

These two views provide a good look at the standard frame canopy in the closed position from the left side. Note the two hinges at the bottom of the center section of the canopy. (Both, Kinzey)

59

The top section of the canopy was hinged on its right side and opened to the position seen here. Note the handle at the center of the left frame. The interior of all of the framework for the windscreen and canopy was painted the same Chromate Green color as the rest of the cockpit. (Kinzey)

Details of the left center section in the fully open position are revealed in these two views. Note the red handle that worked the latch for this section. A smaller handle at the base of the section allowed the forward window portion to be opened. The photo at right provides a good look at the hinges that connected this section to the rest of the canopy and to the fuselage. (Both, Kinzey)

On both the left and right side sections of the canopy, the forward window could be opened by using a small handle and latch at the base of the framework. This is the right side section with that window slid aft to the open position. Note also the small handle on the leading edge of the window that was used to move it forward or aft. (Both, Kinzey)

60

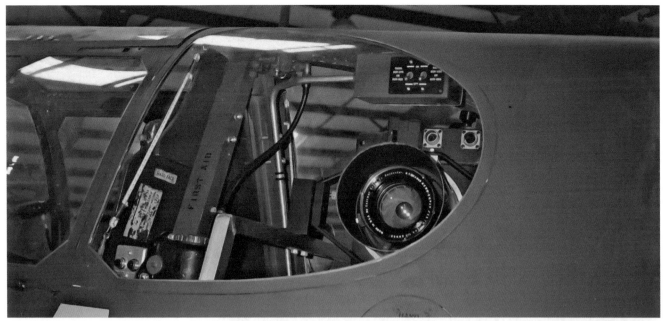

Above and right: These two views provide a good look at the standard rear window on the left side. The rollover structure behind the armor plate in the cockpit is visible through the window. In this case, the camera mounted in the aft cockpit area is small enough that no hole or blister is required for the window. In many cases for F-6A and F-6B photo-recon versions, a round hole was cut in the window. In still other cases for larger cameras, a blistered side window was installed as covered in the P-51-NA, F-6A, & Mustang Mk. IA section of the variants chapter. (Both, Kinzey)

In some cases when small cameras were used, the rear windows were painted over, leaving only a small round area for the camera to take pictures through on the left side. Photo evidence often shows that this area was left open. In at least one case, the opening for a camera was on both rear windows, although it was almost always on the left side as seen here, with the right rear window completely painted over. This practice was usually observed on British photo-recon Mustangs. (Both, Detail & Scale Collection)

PROPELLER DETAILS

Above: All Allison-engined variants of the Mustang were fitted with three-bladed Curtiss Electric propellers. The NA-73X, XP-51, and early British Mustang Mk. Is had propellers that were 10 feet, 6 inches in diameter as seen on this Mustang Mk. I. Operational aircraft had propellers that were painted flat black, but some test aircraft flew with natural metal blades or blades that were painted silver or left natural metal. (NAA via Piet)

Right: During the production of the Mustang Mk. I, the Curtiss Electric propeller was changed to one with a slightly increased diameter of 10 feet, 9 inches, and this would remain standard on all subsequent Allison-powered variants of the Mustang. This view provides a good overall look at the propeller on a restored Mustang, and the Curtis Electric logo is on all three blades. However, vintage photographs clearly show that the logo was not on operational aircraft during World War II. During that time period, propellers on operational Allison-engined Mustangs did have stencils as illustrated in the photographs on the following page. (Manning)

Above: This vintage color photograph of mechanics working on an A-36A shows the Curtiss Electric propeller with the larger diameter as it appeared during World War II. The only markings on the forward side of the blade are the stenciled data and the yellow tips. (G. Balzer Collection)

Right: The three blades of the constant-speed propeller fit into the two-section spinner at its dividing point. Unlike the Hamilton Standard propeller that would follow on the P-51B, C, and D variants, the Curtiss Electric propellers were not cuffed. (Kinzey)

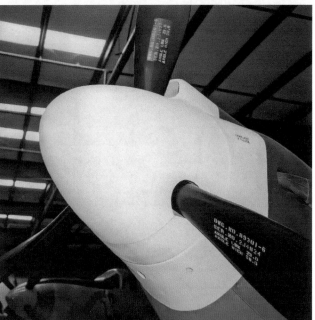

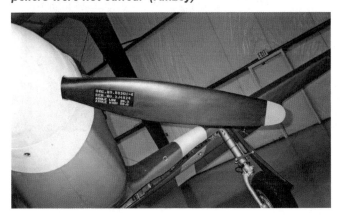

Above: The stenciled data on each blade indicated the drawing number and the serial number of the blade, as well as the low and high pitch angles which were a low of twenty-three degrees and a high of fifty-eight degrees. (Kinzey)

Right: The yellow tip was applied to both sides of each blade, and there was sometimes a small yellow line on the back side of each blade as shown in this photograph. (Kinzey)

63

ALLISON V-1710 ENGINE DETAILS

From the NA-73X prototype through the P-51A, all Mustangs were powered by Allison's V-1710 inline engine. The NA-73X, Mustang Mk. I, XP-51, and the P-51-NA had the V-1710-39, the A-36A was fitted with the V-1710-87, and the V-1710-81 was installed in the P-51A. All were very reliable powerplants that performed well with American fuels. This high view from the left side affords a good look at the details on the top of the engine. (Detail & Scale Collection)

Low side views from the left and right reveal many of the engine's details. Note the six flattened "fishtail" exhaust ports on each side of the engine and the spark plug connections for the cylinders directly below them. The engine block was usually a gray color as seen here. The interior structure was Zinc Chromate Yellow. (Both, Kinzey)

Details on the underside of the engine are visible in this photograph. Numerous lines and wires are visible in this area. (Kinzey)

The engine accessory compartment was located just aft of the engine block. Noteworthy is the Chromate Green air duct that curves down from the long air intake and provides air to the carburetor. The other major item is the oil tank that is Zinc Chromate Yellow. Various linkages, lines, tubes, and wires are also visible. (Both, Kinzey)

FUSELAGE DETAILS

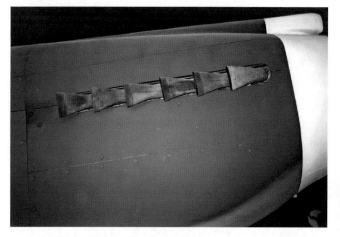

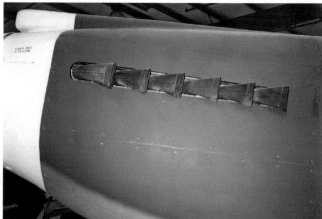

Above, left and right: The forward-most part of the fuse-lage on Allison-powered Mustangs had two major features. The first of these was the long air scoop for carburetor air on top of the cowling. This scoop originally stopped well short of the spinner on the NA-73X proto-type, but it was lengthened to extend forward to immediately aft of the spinner on all subsequent Allison-engined Mustangs. It also became thicker on the A-36A and the P-51A. The six flattened "fishtail" exhaust ports on each side of the cowling comprised the other major feature on the cowling. Also note the door covering the filler for the glycol coolant, visible in the closed position in the photo at right. (Both, Kinzey)

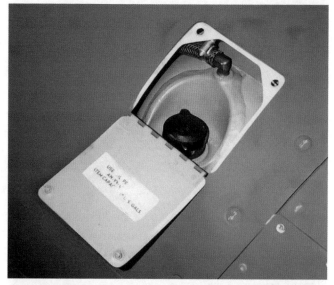

Right: The door that covered the filler for the oil tank was located farther aft on the top of the cowling to the left side. It is shown here in the open position. The tank can be seen in the bottom two photos on the previous page in the Engine Details section. (Kinzey)

The cover for the top of the aft section of the forward fuselage is the subject of these two photographs after it was removed from the aircraft. The access door for the filler for the oil tank is visible and is directly opposite the three vent slots on the right side. (Both, Kinzey)

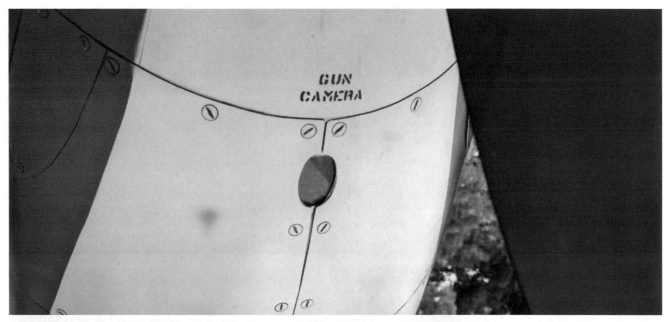

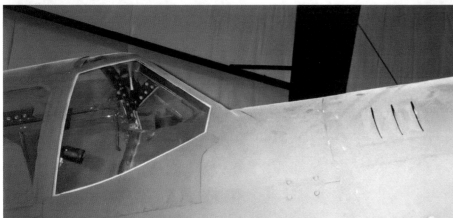

Above: The gun camera was located in the bottom of the forward fuselage on the centerline aft of the spinner. This arrangement was used on the Allison-engined Mustangs, except for early Mustang Mk. Is and the P-51A, both of which had the gun camera in the left wing root. (G. Balzer Collection)

Left: With the cover in place on top of the forward fuselage, the three vents on the right side are visible a little forward of the windscreen. (Kinzey)

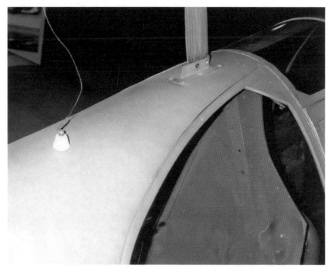

Depending on the radios installed in the aircraft, Allison-powered Mustangs could have differing antenna masts and wiring on the spine of the fuselage just above the radio compartment aft of the seat. A study of the photographs in the variants chapter will reveal several types of masts and wiring configurations. One of the most common is shown here. The masts were sometimes made of wood, because it was a good insulator, and the main wire ran from the top of the mast back to the leading edge of the vertical tail near the top. A vertical wire usually connected the main antenna wire to the radios below, with white insulators being used at each end of the main wire and where the vertical wire entered the fuselage. (Both, Kinzey)

Right: The aircraft's data block was typically stenciled in black one-inch-high letters on the left side of the fuselage, just above the wing root. This was the standard location, but vintage photos sometimes show it in slightly different locations, although it was always on the left side of the fuselage. (Kinzey)

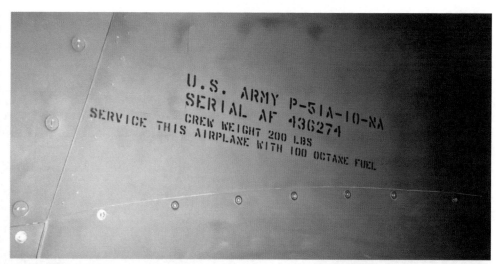

Below center: The hole in the center fuselage on the left side was the port through which the flare pistol could be fired. (Kinzey)

Cooling vents were often located on each side of the aft fuselage behind the radio compartment. These were used to vent heat that was generated by the vacuum tubes in the radios out of the compartment. Some early British Mustang Mk. Is had these vents on top of the fuselage above the radio compartment, as illustrated in a photograph in the Mustang Mk. I section of the variants chapter. (Both, Kinzey)

While the Mustang Mk. I and P-51-NA had shallow hinged radiator scoops under the fuselage (as illustrated in the P-51 section of the variants chapter), the A-36A and P-51A had a shallow fixed scoop as seen here from the left side. The lower cover for the vent area aft of the scoop remained movable. (Kinzey)

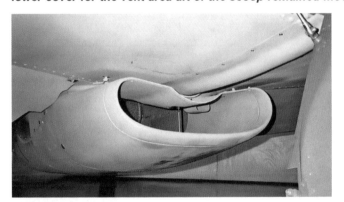

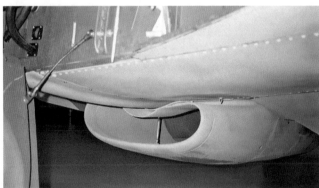

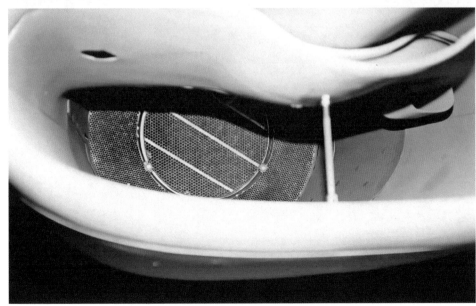

Center, left and right: The shape of the lip of the shallow fixed radiator scoop is revealed in these two photos. Note the dip in the center of the lip at the top that is necessary to clear a longitudinal fairing at the center of the wing structure. There is a small vertical support at the center of the scoop located a little aft of the lip. (Both, Kinzey)

Left: The honeycombed front surface of the circular radiator is visible in this view that looks back inside the fixed shallow scoop. Note also the smaller scoop on the top of the left side of the scoop (to the right in the photograph). (Kinzey)

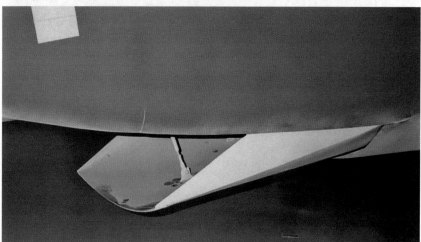

Above: The amount of air flowing through the radiator, and therefore the amount of cooling provided to the Allison engine, was controlled by a large movable vent cover aft of the radiator. It is shown here, along with one of its activating rods, in the open position from the left rear. (Kinzey)

Left: The movable vent cover is illustrated from the right side in this view. It remains in the open position. (Kinzey)

Below: In this photo that looks forward into the vent area, the aft end of the radiator is visible, as are a second activating rod and a structural part of the airframe. (Kinzey)

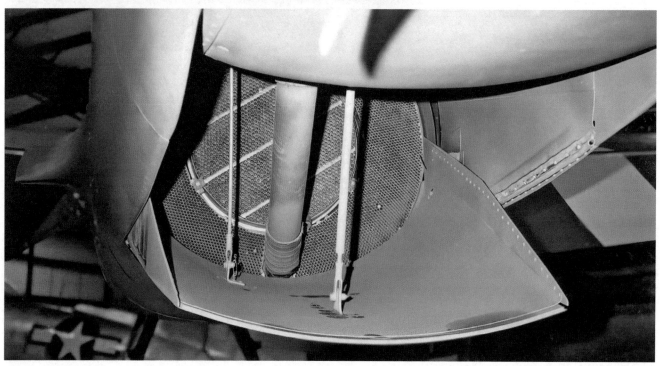

External power could be hooked up to the aircraft under a small rectangular panel just above the trailing edge of the wing flap on the right side of the fuselage. Note the drain just below the wing root on the lower fuselage. A coolant drain was a little farther aft under the fuselage. (Kinzey)

Just above, and slightly forward of the tail landing gear, a tube passed all of the way through the fuselage. A steel bar could be passed through the tube to be used as a hoist point for a crane to lift the aft fuselage and tail section. This was done to provide access inside the tail wheel well and the vent area for the radiator during maintenance, but it was also used to hoist the tail of the aircraft to a level position that was required for boresighting the guns. The hoist point had a capacity of 1,600 pounds. (Kinzey)

WING DETAILS

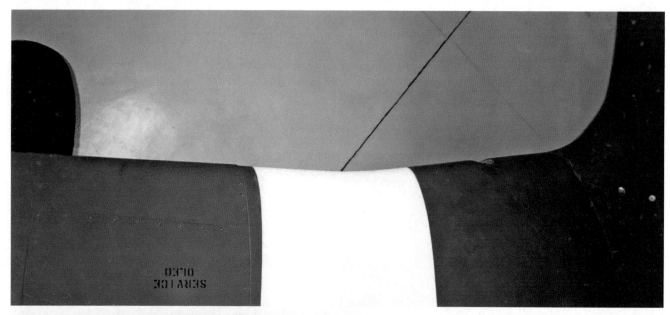

Above: *This photograph looks straight down at the leading edge of the left wing at the root where it meets the fuselage. Note that there is only a very slight curvature forward as the leading edge blends into the fuselage. There is no fillet in this area. The fillet was not added to the wing until production of the P-51D. (Kinzey)*

Left: *The same area of the leading edge of the left wing is shown here from the front. On the P-51A, the gun camera was moved from the bottom of the forward fuselage, where it had been located on the previous variants, except for some early Mustang Mk. Is, to this location in the left wing. Its lens is visible through the small circular opening in the wing. (Kinzey)*

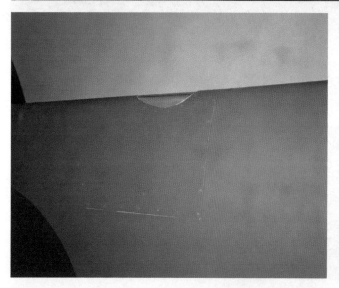

While the Mustang Mk. I, P-51-NA, and Mustang Mk. IA had a single landing light on the leading edge of each wing, and the A-36A had a dual light arrangement on the left wing, the P-51A, F-6B, and Mustang Mk. II had a single light in the leading edge of the left wing only. That light is illustrated in these two photos with the photo at left being taken from above and the one at right being taken from below and outboard of the light. Note that the opening went deeper into the wing on the bottom than on the top. (Both, Kinzey)

 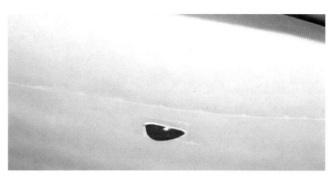

All of the Allison-engine Mustangs had two navigation lights near each wing tip in the form of small teardrop-shaped lights; one on top of the wing and one below it. These red lights were near the tip on the left wing. (Both, Kinzey)

Green navigation lights were on the top and bottom of the right wing near the tip, although they appeared to be blue when not illuminated. Three recognition lights were also under the right wing near the tip, and they were red, amber, and blue/green from front to rear. These lights are visible in the photo at right. (Both, Kinzey)

Above and below: The A-36A and P-51A had a hardpoint under each wing where a rack could be mounted to carry external fuel tanks or bombs up to the 500-pound size. The racks were located just outboard of the machine guns. The rack under the right wing is pictured in the photo above, while the photograph below shows the rack under the left wing. Note the anti-sway braces on both racks. (Both, Kinzey)

With the exception of the A-36A, all Allison-engine Mustangs had an L-shaped pitot probe mounted under the right wing. This would also carry forward on the Rolls-Royce/Packard-engined variants. (Kinzey)

Above and below: All Mustangs had long ailerons that extended from the outboard end of the flaps to just short of the wing tip. The top of the left aileron is shown in these two views. The inboard end of the aileron is visible in the photo below. (Both, Kinzey)

Above: Each aileron had a trim tab located near its inboard end. The actuator was on the underside of the tab. This is the top of the trim tab for the left aileron. (Kinzey)

Right: The entire underside of the left aileron is visible in this photograph. Note that the actuator for the trim tab is located at the outboard edge of the tab. (Kinzey)

Above and below: The right aileron was simply a mirror image of the left aileron. It also had a trim tab near its inboard end. (Both, Kinzey)

Left: As with the left aileron, the actuator for the trim tab on the right aileron was on the bottom at the outboard edge. (Kinzey)

Above: Although the rudder and elevators on early Mustangs were covered in fabric, the ailerons were constructed with a metal skin. Details of the inboard edge of the right aileron are visible in this closeup. (Kinzey)

Above: Mustangs had a large flap on each wing that extended from the root to the inboard edge of the aileron. When the aircraft was on the ground, the flap was usually in the lowered position as seen here. The exposed hinge area at the top was natural metal. Note the numerous flush rivets on top of the flap. (Manning)

Right: Numerous rivets covered the skin on the underside of each flap, although many are difficult to see in this photograph. The straight outboard edge of the left flap is also visible in this photo. (Manning)

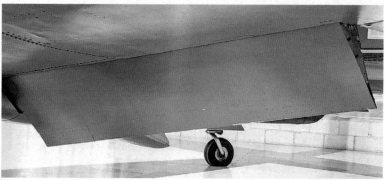

The inboard end for the left flap is viewed from behind in this photograph, and details of the edge are visible. (Kinzey)

The inboard end of each flap was not a straight line, rather it had several angles and curves as revealed in this closeup of the bottom of the left flap. (Kinzey)

The right flap is in the fully lowered position, and from this angle and under these lighting conditions, the numerous flush rivets are clearly visible. (Manning)

Details in the inboard edge of the right flap are revealed inn this photo. They were simply a mirror image of the inboard edge of the left flap. (Kinzey)

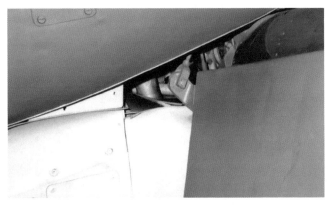

This underside view of the right flap provides a good look at the details on the outboard edge. (Kinzey)

The linkages that operated the flaps were located inside the fuselage and attached to the flap at the top of its inboard edge. This is the linkage connection for the right flap. (Kinzey)

INTERNAL ARMAMENT DETAILS

The Mustang Mk. I had eight machine guns with a mix of four .303-caliber and four .50-caliber weapons. Two of the .50-caliber guns were mounted low in the cowling, with the other six weapons being located in the wings. The P-51-NA and the Mustang Mk. IA had four 20mm cannons in the wings, while the A-36A was armed with six .50-caliber machine guns; two in the cowling and four in the wings as illustrated in the A-36A section of the variants chapter. The internal armament for the P-51A was reduced to only four .50-caliber machine guns mounted in the wings. As illustrated in these two photographs, the weapons were mounted parallel to the ground line, rather than being aligned with the dihedral of the wings. This caused the opening for the muzzle of the outboard gun to be lower than the one for the inboard weapon. (Both, Kinzey)

 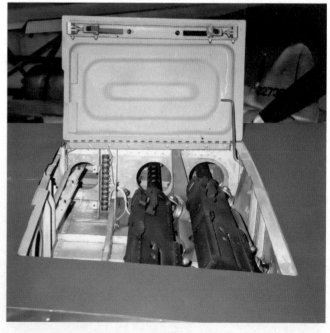

Access to the gun bays and ammunition troughs was provided by one hinged panel and two removable panels. The hinged panel for the left gun bay is shown here in the open position from the front. The panel was hinged at the forward end, and the two latches are visible in the open position. (Kinzey)

The hinged panel for the left gun bay is viewed here from behind. The inside surface was painted Zinc Chromate Yellow. A small rod in the lower right corner holds the panel in the open position. Note how the two guns are mounted at a tilted angle. (Kinzey)

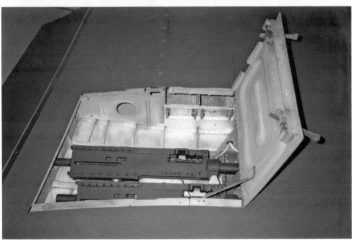

Above: The inboard side of the left gun bay was a solid wall with several stiffeners. The inboard gun was mounted right next to it. On this restored aircraft, the bay itself is left natural metal, and vintage photographs indicate this was often the case on operational aircraft. However, other photos show the Zinc Chromate Primer being applied to the inside of the bay on some aircraft. (Kinzey)

Left: This view reveals the outboard side of the gun bay. While smaller details are not present in this restored P-51A, the major structure of the bay is complete. The rear cover has been removed, but the cover for the ammunition troughs is still in place. The ends of the two ammunition troughs are visible; however, the ammunition feed mechanisms for the guns are not present in this restored aircraft. (Kinzey)

Additional details inside the left gun bay are visible in these two photos. There was always room for a third gun in each bay if the guns had been mounted upright rather than at a tilted angle, although only two were installed in both bays of the A-36A and P-51A. The four-gun arrangement remained unchanged in the later P-51B and P-51C variants. (Both, Kinzey)

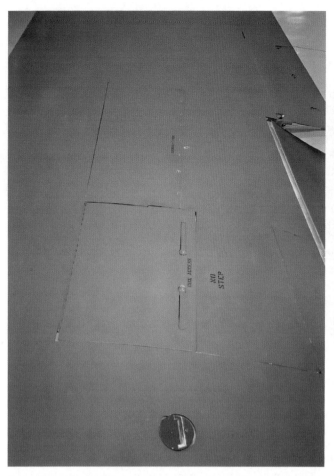

The hinged panel and the two removable panels that cover the right gun bay and ammunition troughs are in the closed position in this photograph. Note the piano hinge on the leading edge of the forward panel. (Kinzey)

The ammunition troughs for the right side guns are visible in this photograph. Up to 325 rounds could be loaded for each weapon, and this load provided twenty-one seconds of firing time. Note the circular lightening holes in the aft wall of the rear trough. The holes for the fasteners along the trailing edge of the covering panel are also visible. The fact that there was room for a third gun is again apparent in this photo. (Kinzey)

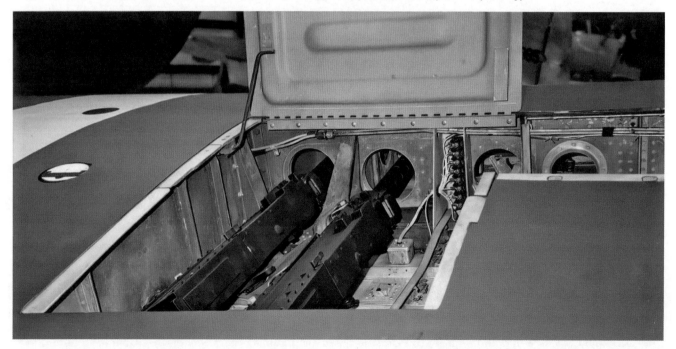

This low view provides a good look at the holes through which the barrels of the machine guns extend forward to the leading edge of the wings. Again, note that the guns are tilted so that their tops are facing at an outward angle. The inside surface of the piano hinge for the forward cover is also visible. (Kinzey)

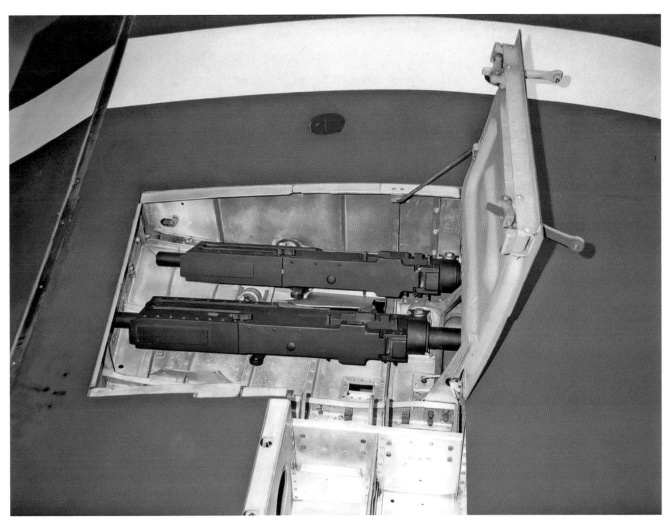

The inboard side of each gun bay was just outboard of the fuel tank in the wing. The red filler cap for the tank is visible just inboard of the gun bay. (Kinzey)

Circular lightening holes were present along the wall of the forward ammunition trough. The forward end of the covering panel slipped under a lip above the wall, and fasteners were only used along the trailing edge of the cover. (Kinzey)

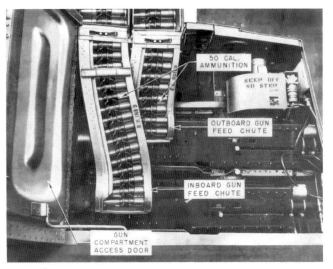

Because the ammunition feed chutes are not in place on the restored P-51A in the other photos in this section, this photograph from the maintenance manual is included to illustrate details of the feed chutes and how they fed the .50-caliber ammunition to the two guns in the right wing. The arrangement for the left guns would simply be a mirror image of what is shown here. (NMUSAF)

LANDING GEAR DETAILS

All of the Allison-powered Mustangs had the same landing gear, and this would remain unchanged through the P-51B, P-51C, and P-51D that followed. Details of the left landing gear are illustrated in these two views. Vintage color photos from the World War II period indicate that the inside surface of the outer main gear doors was silver in some cases, but in other photographs they appear to be Chromate Green as seen in the photo at left. Note the details on the outside of the main gear wheel in the photo at right. (Left, Kinzey; Right, Manning)

Left: The struts were painted a flat silver or steel color. The correct angle of the outer door in relation to the strut is visible in this front view of the left landing gear. Note also the forward brace that attaches the door to the strut. (Kinzey)

Above: This closeup provides a good look at the inside of the main gear wheel and how the single-fork strut attaches to it. A hydraulic line ran down along the aft side of the fork to the brake assembly at the center of the wheel. (Kinzey)

Most of the interior of the gear well for the left landing gear is visible in this photograph that looks outward toward the strut. Original color photos from the World War II indicate that the wells were painted Chromate Green on the early Mustang variants as seen here, although this would later be changed to Zinc Chromate Yellow. (Kinzey)

The inner surface of the inboard main gear door was usually painted Chromate Green, but often the center area was left natural metal. The actuator for the door was in the upper forward corner, and there was a flexible cable connector at the upper aft corner. On the Allison-engined Mustangs, these inner doors usually remained in the closed position when the aircraft was on the ground; however, they could be opened to provide access for maintenance. (Kinzey)

Plumbing, tubes, and various lines were located in the inboard end of each main wheel well. In the left inboard gear well, the big line carried cool ethylene glycol up to the header tank from the radiator, and the small one was the cool aftercoolant supply heading toward the aftercooler header tank. Again, note the silver actuator at the upper forward corner of the door, and the flexible cable connection at the aft upper corner. The curved forward edge of the well was very close to the leading edge of the wing on all Mustang variants up through the P-51C. Among the Allison-powered Mustangs, access to the gun camera, located in the leading edge of the left wing near the root on the P-51A, was provided through the left main gear well. (Kinzey)

Top left and above: The right landing gear was simply a mirror image of the left. In the photo at left, note that there is a small tab at the very top of the outer door. There was a small recessed edge at the very bottom of the outer door that fit under the edge of the inner door when the gear was retracted. On the main gear struts, the scissors link for the oleo portion of the gear extended aft. The spoked outside surface of the main gear wheel is also visible. (Both, Kinzey)

Left: The brake assembly on the inside surface of each main gear caused the openings in the wheel to be different on the inside surface than they were on the outside of the wheel. Several different tread designs on the tires could be found on Mustangs, but most had the diamond tread seen here. This was particularly true of the early Allison-powered variants. (Kinzey)

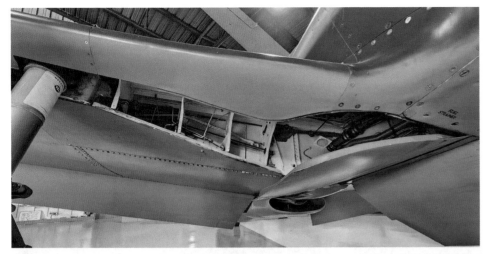

Taken from in front of the wing and looking aft, this view provides a good look at the aft wall of the right landing gear well. Although it is painted white, rather than the correct Chromate Green color on this restored P-51A, the physical details, including the various lines and linkages, are correct. What is most important in this photograph is that the aft wall of the well is not flush with the opening for the well itself. Rather it is recessed back from the opening inside of the wing structure. (Manning)

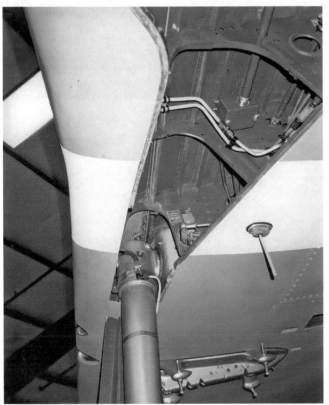

Center left and right: Additional details inside the right main gear well are visible in these two photographs. Note how the main gear strut attaches to the structure of the wing at the outer end of the wheel well. (Both, Kinzey)

Left: The inside surface of the inboard main gear door is the subject of this photo. Again, the actuator is in the upper forward corner, and there is a flexible cable connector at the upper aft corner. There is an unpainted center area. Vintage photographs show this feature on some Mustangs but not on others. In the background to the right, the hydraulic line leading down to the brake assembly on the left landing gear is visible. (Kinzey)

The tail landing gear was fully retractable on all Mustang variants, and when closed, two rectangular-shaped doors cover the well. In the photo at left, the right side of the tail wheel is visible, illustrating its six small holes. It was connected to a single fork on the strut. The photograph at right shows the left side of the tail wheel; however, it should be noted that the photo was taken from the right side of the aircraft. This is because the tail wheel castored around 180 degrees when the aircraft was pushed back into its position inside the hangar. (Left, Manning; right Kinzey)

Left: Details of the strut and much of the tail gear well is visible in this photograph that looks up and aft into the well. The well was simply the interior of the aft fuselage. Note the steering mechanism for the tail landing gear. (Kinzey)

Above: The inside surfaces of the two tail wheel doors were painted Chromate Green, as was the case on the main gear doors. This photo was taken from behind the tail landing gear and looks forward. The actuators were attached near the aft end of each door. The oleo portion of the forked-shaped aft part of the strut assembly is also visible. (Kinzey)

TAIL DETAILS

Above: This is the empennage on the NA-73X prototype. Its design would remain basically unchanged through the P-51D variant. It was a metal structure with fabric covering the rudder and elevators. (NAA via Piet)

Right: An overall view of the left side of the vertical tail reveals the full height rudder with its large external counterbalance near the top of the hinge line and the large trim tab along the trailing edge. (Kinzey)

The actuator for the large trim tab was at the base of the tab on the right side of the rudder. (Kinzey)

A small white navigation light was located low on the trailing edge of the rudder. This feature was on all Mustang variants. (Kinzey)

Above: The horizontal tail was a conventional design, consisting of a horizontal stabilizer and a full-span elevator with an external mass balance. It was mounted high on the aft fuselage at zero degrees of dihedral. (Kinzey)

Left: Each fabric-covered elevator had a large metal trim tab on its trailing edge. On the left horizontal tail, the actuator for the trim tab was on the undersurface. (Kinzey)

Below: An underside look at the lower surface of the left horizontal tail reveals the actuator for the trim tab at its center. (Kinzey)

The horizontal tails were identical so that they could be mounted on either side of the aircraft, and this meant that the actuator for the trim tab on the right elevator was on the upper surface. (Kinzey)

An overall look at the underside of the right horizontal tail is provided in this photograph. (Kinzey)

MODELERS SECTION

Allison-powered Mustangs have not been well represented in kit form over the years. While none are truly excellent and state-of-the-art, with some work correcting inaccuracies and adding details, reasonably good results can be obtained. In this photograph, the three 1/72nd scale models in front are the Italeri P-51-NA, the M News A-36A, and the Frog P-51A. Behind them is the ICM 1/48th scale P-51A. (Kinzey)

Note: Each volume in the Detail & Scale Series has a Modelers Section in the back of the publication that includes reviews of the injection-molded plastic kits of the subject aircraft. Resin kits are sometimes included if there is no injection molded kit of a specific variant of the subject aircraft. All standard scales are included. Highlights, limitations, and recommendations are considered with respect to which kits in each scale are the best for the scale modeler. One should compare the features of a kit to the detailed photographs in the book to determine how accurately and extensively they are represented. The modeler can then decide what, if any, work to undertake to enhance the appearance and accuracy of the model.

In this section, the reader will find reviews of injection molded Allison-powered P-51s up through the P-51A and their derivatives. Kits of the P-51B/C and later variants are covered in **P-51 Mustang in Detail & Scale, Part 2,** and the P-51D/K through P-51H are examined in **P-51 Mustang in Detail & Scale, Part 3.** Because space is limited, some older, long-out-of production, and lower-quality kits are not covered. Also not covered are kits of early Mustangs converted into post-war racers (e.g., Civilized Models, High Planes Models). We do refer readers to the Scale Modeling Section of our website at https://detailandscale.com for reviews of more recent P-51 aftermarket items.

1/144th SCALE KITS

Unfortunately, no kits of the Allison-powered Mustang variants have been produced by model manufacturers in 1/144th scale. Hopefully, this will be corrected in the future.

1/72nd SCALE KITS

Older Kits

For many years, model manufacturers all but ignored the Allison-engined Mustangs. What was available were crude limited-production kits that were plagued with inaccuracies and lacked detailing. One such example in 1/72nd scale was from Frog, and it was the first kit in this popular scale that represented an Allison-engined variant. It was very poor by today's standards, and there were numerous inaccuracies. It was actually difficult to tell exactly which version of the Mustang Frog was trying to represent. No armament was represented, and that basically leaves out the P-51 or Mustang Mk. IA with the large 20mm cannon. Likewise, there were no chin guns provided, so the Mustang Mk. I and A-36 can be eliminated. Since this clearly is an Allison-engined Mustang, the only remaining possibility is the P-51A. But there is scribing for landing/taxi lights on the leading edges of both wings, and that is not correct for the P-51A.

For many years, this was the only 1/72nd scale kit of an Allison-engined Mustang, and modelers had to do a lot of work to correct its multiple inaccuracies and to add a reasonable amount of detailing. But today, much better kits are available in 1/72nd scale, and the Frog kit only has value to collectors.

Other older kits were released by M News, a model manufacturer from the Czech Republic. One of their first kits was a limited production 1/72nd scale A-36. This model was rather rudimentary, and parts were covered with flash. It was poorly engineered, and at first glance it might not seem worth build-

Two of the older 1/72ⁿᵈ scale kits of Allison-powered Mustangs include the Frog P-51A at left and the M News A-36A Apache at right. Both of these kits required a lot of work correcting inaccuracies, substituting of parts from other kits, and adding details to achieve the results seen here. Better models of the subjects are now available in 1/72ⁿᵈ scale, although none are truly excellent. (Both, Kinzey)

ing. But the shapes are generally correct, and surprisingly the panel lines are engraved. This allows for considerable sanding which is necessary during construction. The flash makes many of the small parts unusable, and this is probably just as well, because most of them are crude and inaccurate.

When we decided to build this kit years ago, we used only the fuselage halves, the tops and bottom of the wings, the rudder, horizontal stabilizers, spinner, and propeller. Almost all of the other parts, to include the landing gear, exhausts, cockpit interior, radio antenna mast, pylons, and hot air ramp, were taken from a Hasegawa P-51B. Bombs came from a Monogram P-51B, while the chin guns were found in the spares box. The pitot probe was made from a straight pin, and the clear cover for the dual landing/taxi lights was made from a piece of a clear toothbrush.

During basic construction, we cut the main gear wells out of the lower wing of the Hasegawa kit. With some trimming, we got this to fit inside the wings of the M News kit. We also added the Hasegawa hot air ramp to the underside of the fuselage, and we used the Hasegawa tail wheel in place of the one provided in the M News kit. Inside the cockpit, we used several of the parts from the Hasegawa kit as well as making some details from scratch. With a little trimming, the thin, clear, Hasegawa canopy can be made to fit this kit, thus replacing the thicker and rather cloudy one that M News provides.

M News also released the Mustang Mk. I and Mustang Mk. IA in a single kit. This kit was essentially the same as the A-36, and it required the same extra work as described above. The bombs, included in the A-36 kit, have appropriately been deleted, but the pylons remain. The instructions show these pylons being added under the wings, but neither the Mustang Mk. I nor the Mustang Mk. IA were fitted with them. Two pairs of 20mm cannon were added for use with the Mustang Mk. IA.

These limited production M News kits leave a lot to be desired, and fortunately better options are now available for these Mustang variants in 1/72ⁿᵈ scale.

Italeri P-51 & P-51A

Italeri has issued several 1/72ⁿᵈ scale kits of Mustangs, and these include the P-51-NA, Mustang Mk. I, and P-51A variants among the versions equipped with Allison engines. The first of these was released in 1998 as a P-51-NA, and it was re-issued again in 2010. A P-51A kit followed in 2022. These are essentially the same kit with parts to build the respective variant represented. None are currently in production as of the release date of this publication in early 2025, but they can be found at online auction sites and at model shows.

While certainly better than the previous Frog and M News kits, the Italeri early Mustangs still left a lot to be desired. In the first two issues, the model could be built as a P-51-NA with the four 20mm cannon or as a Mustang Mk. I. For the Mustang Mk. I, optional parts were provided for the six wing guns to be used in place of the four 20mm cannon. The two cowl-mounted machine guns that were standard on the Mustang Mk. I were also included, but they were mounted directly to the cowling without the noticeable fairing where the barrels exited the cowling as found on the Mustang Mk. I. By using the four 20mm cannons, a Mustang Mk. IA could also be built, if the modeler could find aftermarket decals to use as markings.

The wrong wing was provided which had the fillet at the leading edge of each wing root. This feature did not appear on any variant until the P-51D. Fortunately, there was enough plastic forward of the main wheel wells to allow the modeler to remove the fillet and produce the correct leading edge.

When building a P-51-NA with the four 20mm cannons, another problem with the wing was that the landing lights just outboard of the cannons were not represented, so spaces for these had to be cut into the leading edge, and the covers could then be added with some Krystal Klear or clear plastic. Likewise, the two landing lights for the Mustang Mk. I were also not included in the leading edge of the wing. Again, these had to be added by cutting into the leading edge of each wing in the

appropriate locations, then adding Krystal Klear or clear plastic. The instructions tell the modeler to use the landing light that goes in the left landing gear, but this is not correct for any version prior to the P-51D.

The flaps were molded integral to the wings. In building our review sample, we cut the flaps away from the wings, assembled them separately, added the forward edge with plastic card stock, and set them aside to be added later in the lowered position as they most commonly would be on a Mustang sitting on the ground.

The panel lines and surface details were engraved, but they were not complete or entirely accurate. The ailerons lacked trim tabs. The engraved framework on the canopy was also incomplete, and the canopy itself was poorly designed, having part of the fuselage molded to the aft windows. Unless individual sections of the canopy were cut apart by the modeler, the canopy could only be added in the closed position. The cockpit detail was minimal, and there were no details at all on the sides of the cockpit. The control column was noticeably too tall and had to be cut down to the correct height.

The kits came with pylons to go under the wings, and options for 75-gallon fuel tanks or 500-pound bombs were provided to go on them. However, the P-51-NA and Mustang Mk. I and Mk. IA did not have the pylons or the capability to carry these underwing stores.

When the P-51A kit was released, the wing armament was changed to the four .50-caliber machine guns. For this kit, the pylons and either the bombs or fuel tanks could be used. All other issues covered above still remained in this release.

By correcting the inaccuracies, adding some detailing in the cockpit, and adding the appropriate landing lights, a reasonable shelf model of an Allison-engined Mustang could be built using one of the Italeri kits, but the Academy and Brengun kits reviewed next are better options.

Academy P-51-NA

After Academy released a 1/72nd scale P-51B in 1999, it followed with a P-51C in 2003. This line was the basis for a third release of a P-51-NA the following year. The P-51-NA kit differs from the first two in that Academy provides new fuselage halves with the Allison engine nose section, wings with the 20mm cannon barrels, the three-bladed propeller, and other items. Parts breakdown is simple, and it is generally a well-fitting, straightforward kit consisting of forty-nine parts with an additional forty-eight parts for the optional ground equipment. Underwing stores add another fifteen parts to the total count.

This kit gets the basics correct for the P-51-NA, including the nose and cowling shape, the long carburetor air intake,

radiator inlet style, and the four wing cannons. Rivet details on the wings are mostly absent from the forward forty percent of the wing surfaces, and all the important larger fasteners are present on the fuselage and cowlings.

There is an acceptable level of cockpit detail for 1/72nd scale, though a close inspection reveals a simplified instrument panel, a slightly misshapen pilot's seat, and inaccurate sidewall details. Standard and Malcolm hood canopies are provided. Builders have an option for shrouded or unshrouded exhaust stacks and two styles of radio masts. The landing gear and wheels are well done, and the wheel wells have good basic structural detail. Yet, the main gear wells are strikingly shallow. Main gear well doors are well detailed, but the inner surface door detail is too highly elevated. The spaces behind the landing light covers are open to the interior of the wing as no actual landing light is provided. The underwing shell ejector ports are present, but the two link ejector ports on each side are missing.

Generally, these errors or omissions are relatively minor and easily correctable. If one is looking for a straightforward build, and if detail oversights are not a concern, Academy's P-51-NA is recommended. However, the kit is no longer in production, and it is difficult to find one at an online auction site and at model shows.

Brengun Mustang Mk. I, P-51-NA/Mustang Mk. IA, A-36 Apache, and A-36 Apache RAF Markings

Brengun is a Czech model company that released a line of Allison-powered Mustang kits between 2017 and 2019. They share nearly all the same parts, and we will briefly evaluate their A-36 kits separately below. They are relatively simple kits with a low parts count and a conventional parts breakdown. Panel lines are crisp and recessed. Recessed rivet detail is minimal and it mostly represents the engine cowling DZUS fasteners. The quality of the kit is typical for a limited run, low-pressure injection molded kit. There are no locating pins, so fit and parts alignment can be challenging, and we recommend making your own locating tabs using plastic sheet or rod.

Unfortunately, the kit has a major inaccuracy. The fuselage is noticeably too deep for an Allison-powered Mustang. Instead, it has the contours of the taller fuselage like the one used on the later Merlin-engined variants. This is impossible to correct using only kit parts.

There are not many construction options, but the flaps are separate and can be displayed in the lowered position. The left half of the radiator inlet is short-shot, and the right half is filled with plastic, indicating that the mold was leaky. This seems to have been a known issue, so Brengun includes a far better cast resin radiator inlet replacement part to be used instead.

Cockpit detail is adequate. The curved floor of an Allison-powered Mustang is present. The instrument panel has raised detail, and the pilot's seat is passable. Sidewall details are present, and while the detail is soft, much of this will be hard to see once the single-piece windscreen/canopy combination is installed. A camera is included to build any of the early reconnaissance Mustangs, but the modeler will have to drill a hole through the left side window to represent an RAF recce version. Wide and narrow carburetor inlets are included, but the inlet is solid plastic and needs to be drilled out.

One highlight is a very nicely detailed main wheel well, though the back of the wheel well incorrectly follows the profile of the rear landing gear well opening in the lower wing. There are scribed panel lines for the underwing shell ejection ports, but they are of an incorrect configuration.

The Brengun A-36 kits feature newly tooled upper and lower wing halves with correct dive brake wells. The dive brakes themselves are very well represented by photoetched parts. At this time, this kit may be the easiest route to build a 1/72nd scale A-36, representing the only choice outside of the long unavailable M News kit covered under Older Kits above. However, the incorrect fuselage found in all of the Brengun kits is a major inaccuracy. The only way to correct this is to use the fuselage from an Academy P-51-NA and mate the Brengun A-36A wings to it. Because of the inaccurate fuselage, we cannot recommend the Brengun kits.

Gartex P-51A Mustang

This now defunct Japanese manufacturer with ties to Hasegawa produced a limited run P-51A kit in 1994. Today, it is very hard to find, but it is worth a brief discussion here. This kit is essentially a conversion set to backdate the Hasegawa P-51B/C kit to a P-51A. Gartex includes the complete set of Hasegawa P-51B/C sprues in their boxing, but it also includes cast resin fuselage halves with the Allison engine nose. White

Brengun's family of 1/72nd scale Allison-powered Mustangs includes the Mustang I, the P-51-NA/Mustang 1A, and the A-36A. However, they have a major inaccuracy with the forward fuselage which is the deeper design found on the Merlin-engined variants. To correct this problem, Paul Boyer used the fuselage from an Academy P-51-NA and mated the wings from Brengun A-36A to build this model. (Boyer)

metal parts allow the builder to represent the experimental landing ski configuration.

P-51A details, such as the .50-caliber machine guns, the wider carburetor air scoop, early underwing pylons, and the fixed radiator inlet scoop appear to be well represented. Some builders have reported that the cast resin fuselage halves are thin to the point that they are significantly warped in some kits. Yet, the biggest problem, and potentially a game-ender for many scale modelers, is the inclusion of Hasegawa's P-51B/C wings. Hasegawa made an infamous mistake here by copying the planform of the P-51D wing with the large fillet on each leading edge at the root. This fillet was not present on any early Mustangs. This mistake is both glaring and something that cannot be fixed by sanding down the leading-edge fillet, since the overly shallow main gear well extends into the fillet. We discuss this issue with the Hasegawa P-51B/Cs further in the Modeler's Section of *P-51 Mustang in Detail & Scale, Part 2.*

In summary, today this kit is extremely rare and expensive if one can find it, and it features a major accuracy error. It has been eclipsed by the Academy and Brengun P-51s, which are where scale modelers should choose to invest their effort and money.

MPM A-36A, P-51-NA/Mustang Mk. IA, and P-51-NA/F-6A

MPM issued a small line of early Allison-powered Mustangs between 1995 and 1999, and these subsequently appeared under Směr and Special Hobby labels. These are comparable to the more recent Brengun kits as limited run, low-pressure, injection molded kits. Surfaces of the fuselage and wings can be somewhat irregular and need to be sanded smooth. There are large sprue gates connecting to the parts that require careful removal and additional cleanup. Basic

mounting pins help align the fuselage and wing halves, but there are no mounting tabs for the horizontal stabilizers. Flash is found on many parts. Panel lines are recessed, and only the largest fasteners are represented. Cast resin detail parts accompany the sprues.

The MPM kits look like a Mustang in terms of overall shapes and sizes, though the upper part of the engine nacelle is vertically shortened, but this is nearly imperceptible. The kit has two cockpit construction options. One uses the injection-molded cockpit parts that are devoid of almost all detail. The other option builds up out of the kit's twelve cast resin parts. These include the cockpit floor, the sidewalls, the pilot's seat, an oblique camera, radio set, control column, gunsight, and instrument panel. These parts look very good for 1/72nd scale, though the cockpit floor is flat instead of curved. The canopy and windscreen are a single piece, and the bulged left side window for the camera is a separate part.

There are numerous problem areas with these kits. The front of the carburetor air inlet is solid plastic and needs to be opened up. The main landing gear well is far too shallow in terms of vertical and aft depth, and it is excessively curved in cross-section. While wheels are provided on the sprues, the cast resin wheels are far superior, and there is no question as to which ones to use. Shell and link ejection ports are missing on the underside of the wings. The landing light in the forward left wing is present, but the light on the right side is absent. Plastic parts are provided for the radiator inlet, but their openings are partially obscured by thick flash. A pair of very inaccurate bombs are included as the only external stores option.

The plastic parts in the MPM Allison-powered Mustangs are not particularly comparable to today's kits, especially with better options available. However, if one wishes to build one of MPM's kits, the cast resin parts add valuable enhancement. We do not recommend these kits.

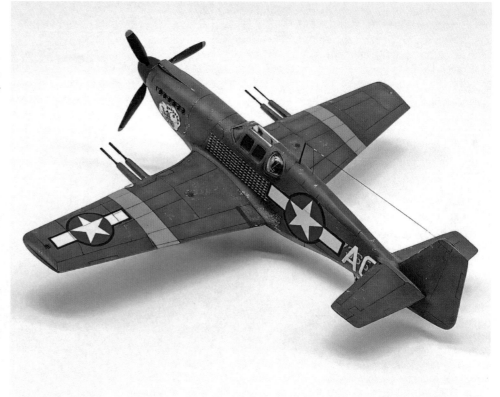

The MPM family of 1/72nd scale Allison-powered Mustangs are typical of 1990s-era limited run, low-pressure, injection molded kits. Many parts require extensive cleanup. Careful attention to fit can produce a good model in this scale, though more modern kits from Brengun feature better detail and accuracy. Co-author Haagen Klaus built the MPM F-6A out-of-the-box, and it has the markings for a Mustang flown by the "Snoopers" of the 111th Tactical Reconnaissance Squadron in the spring of 1943 while operating in Algeria. (Klaus)

1/48th SCALE KITS

Accurate Miniatures, Italeri, Academy, and Premium Hobby P-51-NA, P-51A, Mustang Mk. IA, F-6A, and F-6B, and A-36A

In 1994, Accurate Miniatures released three 1/48th scale Allison-powered Mustangs as their first kits. These were of the P-51-NA, P-51A, and A-36A. They were followed by a British Mustang Mk. IA in 1995. Between 2013 and 2020, they were sold under the Italeri, Academy, and Premium Hobby labels. Below, we review the P-51-NA and the common tooling between them all before describing features of different variants.

These kits are well researched, well detailed, and very accurate. They are not over-engineered and average around seventy-eight parts. Surface details are represented by fine recessed panel lines. Raised rivets are present, but they are in scale and are found only where they are on the real aircraft. Fit is very good, and *generally* only a small amount of filling and sanding is required. Still, these kits have also developed a reputation for tricky nose-to-fuselage and fuselage-to-wing alignments followed by seam filling. Test fitting will help avoid any major problems.

The cockpit is well detailed, and the floor is correctly represented as the curved top of the center wing section in the Allison-powered Mustangs. Cockpit side details are separate pieces. The instrument panel is a clear part, and the builder may simply paint the part black and apply a decal, or by leaving the "glass" on the instruments clear and apply the decal to the back of the panel to show through the clear instrument face. One small problem involves the recoils on the 20mm cannon being marginally oversized. A little sanding will correct this. Also, none of the control surfaces are positionable and everything is molded in the neutral position. This means that the modeler must do some plastic surgery if the flaps are to be mounted in the lowered position as they normally would be when the aircraft was on the ground. We consider this to be one of the three shortcomings of these kits.

The landing gear is well detailed. A deep main gear well is molded integrally into the bottom wing piece. A problem area here is that because the main gear wells are molded as part of the lower wings, this means that the walls are even with the openings for the wells. The rear wall, in particular, should be recessed aft into the wing structure. A feature that modelers will appreciate is that the wheels and the tires are separate pieces, which makes painting a breeze if one is not using masks. Round and slightly flattened tires are included.

The clear parts sprue is common to all kits, and it includes two windscreens, standard and Malcolm hood canopies, rear cockpit windows, and all the landing lights for the different versions. The reason for the two windscreens is that many A-36s and P-51As had a small window on the left panel. One of the windscreens has this panel, while the other does not. Given such attention to detail, it is unfortunate that neither the standard nor the Malcolm canopies can be displayed in the open position as they come in the kit. This is what we consider to be the second of the three shortcomings of these kits. The standard canopy can be cut with a razor saw and assembled in the open position, but the Malcolm hood is not wide enough to fit over the fuselage and rear windows. One solution involves stealing a Malcolm hood from a Monogram, Tamiya, or Eduard P-51B/C kit. However, compared to the P-51B and P-51C that

Although they were first released three decades ago, the Accurate Miniatures kits of the Allison-engine Mustangs in 1/48th scale remain the best available today of those early Mustang variants in any scale. They are now issued under the Academy label. This is the original Accurate Miniatures P-51-NA model built by Stan Parker not long after the kits were first issued. (Parker)

followed, relatively few of the Allison-engined Mustangs were field-fitted with the Malcolm hood, so there won't be many models that require them. The lack of an open position option for the standard framed canopy remains a more important shortcoming of these kits.

The third shortcoming is the instruction sheet. It is quite poorly drawn and difficult to follow, particularly for the landing gear. The exact place where some of the parts join is unclear. In later kits, professionally rendered instructions replaced this first generation of instructions.

Accurate Miniatures P-51-NA, Mustang Mk. IA, F-6A, & F-6B

These kits are virtually the same as the kit covered immediately above, but it is molded in light gray plastic. The

F-6A and F-6B kits were latecomers to the Accurate Miniatures catalog being released in 2005 and 2003, respectively. A few extra parts provide a different aft cockpit deck and a camera installation. There is also a rear-view mirror to go atop the windscreen frame. The sprue of clear parts has an extra left rear cockpit window with a hole for the camera. These parts could also be swapped with the P-51-NA and P-51A kits to build USAAF F-6A and F-6B photo-recon variants as well.

Accurate Miniatures P-51A

Different wings come in this kit with the appropriate changes required for the P-51A. These include the single landing/taxi light on the left wing and the four machine guns in place of the 20mm cannons. The correct shell ejection chutes are on the underside of the wings, but there is only one of the two

Above: Stan Parker also built this model of a P-51A using the initial Accurate Miniatures release of that variant. The markings are those of the Mustang flown by Lieutenant Sid Newcomb while he was assigned to the 530th Fighter Squadron of the 311th Fighter Group. (Parker)

Left: This A-36A was built by Rick Troutman using the Accurate Miniatures kit. One of shortcomings of the Accurate Miniatures/ Academy kits is the fact that the flaps are molded integral to the wings, thus requiring plastic surgery to display them in the lowered position as they typically would be with the aircraft sitting on the ground. Another is that there is no option to display the canopy in the open position. To do so requires having to carefully cut the individual sections of the canopy apart. (Troutman)

link chutes under each wing. The barrels of the machine guns are separate pieces that fit in the holes in the leading edge of the wing. This is a better arrangement than having the barrels molded inside the holes or left out entirely. Underwing pylons can mount a pair of 75-gallon external fuel tanks. The scoop for the cooling air intake is correct for the P-51A in that it does not have the panel lines of the hinged inlet. The carburetor scoop is wider than those provided in the P-51-NA and Mustang Mk. IA kits, indicating the presence of an air filter. For most P-51As, the windscreen with the small window in the left panel should be used. Carefully check your reference material as to which windscreen is appropriate for the specific aircraft you are modeling.

Accurate Miniatures A-36

The A-36 features many new parts, although the basics remain the same. The wings have the dive brakes molded into the wing surfaces. It is truly unfortunate that these were not separate pieces to give the builder the option of either extended or retracted dive brakes. The spaces between the vanes of the dive brakes are open as they should be, but the dive brake wells are absent. This means you can see through the hollow wing between the upper and lower dive brakes. Just glue a piece of thin plastic card on the inside of the wing under the brake to eliminate this problem.

The dual landing/taxi light is correctly represented in the leading edge of the left wing. The pitot boom is included to go in the hole in the leading edge of the right wing. The four wing guns are the same as found in the P-51A kit. The two nose parts for the fuselage are also different, in that they have the holes for the chin-mounted machine guns. The guns themselves are simply barrels which push back into the holes and meet a stop. The carburetor scoop is the correct wider variety. Like the P-51A, the A-36 kit has underwing pylons, but instead of external fuel tanks, two 250-pound bombs are provided. These are very well executed, and each consists of six pieces.

As of this writing, three decades have passed since the first Accurate Miniatures release of an Allison-powered Mustang. On one hand, these kits generally stand up to the test of time. On the other hand, they do not compare as well to today's state-of-the-art kits. We recommend these kits as the best in Allison-powered Mustangs in 1/48th scale.

ICM P-51A, Mustang Mk. II, and F-6B

ICM is a model company in Ukraine that is producing a wide range of plastic model kits. In 2004 they released a 1/48th scale model of the P-51A, and this was followed by releases of a USAAF F-6A reconnaissance variant and then a British Mustang Mk. II, also equipped with cameras. Another release of a P-51A followed a couple of years thereafter. Essentially all of these kits were exactly the same, featuring optional parts to build the variant depicted in the box art, and the decals were also changed to build those versions. These Allison-engined Mustang kits fit into a larger collection of ICM Mustangs in 1/48th scale that included P-51B, P-51C, and P-51D variants as well as their British counterparts. For the Allison-powered Mustangs, ICM only offered the P-51A and the corresponding F-6A and Mustang Mk. II photo-recon versions. They have not produced a Mustang Mk. I, P-51-NA, a Mustang Mk. IA, or an A-36A.

These are limited production kits, having no pins and holes to line things up, so extra care has to be taken during assembly. There is flash on some parts, but it is minimal and easily removed. As with most limited production kits, the places where parts are joined to the sprues are rather heavy, and this requires cleanup of the parts before assembly to ensure a good fit. Overall, the fit is generally good, except where the wing assembly joins the fuselage. This requires some extra test fitting, some reshaping of the top of the wheel wells, and some filling and sanding to get it to look right. Surface detailing is recessed and reasonably well done, although not completely accurate.

The flaps are molded as separate parts, and this makes positioning them in the lowered position a simple matter. This is one place that the ICM kits are better than those from Accurate Miniatures. However, this advantage is countered by the fact that the wings have the fillet at the leading edge of the root, and this is incorrect. Fortunately, there is enough plastic

The author used the ICM kit to build this P-51A, representing the aircraft flown by Captain J. J. England while he was commander of the 530th Fighter Squadron of the 311th Fighter Group at Dinjan, China, in May 1944. While not quite as good as the Accurate Miniatures kits, this is still a reasonably good kit, and it has the advantage of having the flaps as separate parts that can easily be displayed in the lowered position. The biggest drawbacks are the terrible instructions and the very poor decals. (Kinzey)

forward of the wheel wells to allow the modeler to remove the fillets and rework the leading edge of each wing root to the correct shape for the earlier Mustang variants. On the plus side, the four machine guns are mounted in the wings correctly, being parallel to the ground, rather than aligned with the dihedral of the wings.

The inner main gear doors on the early Mustangs usually remained in the closed position when the aircraft was on the ground, and getting these doors to fit properly in the closed position will take some sanding along the leading edge. This is because the lip inside the wheel well where the forward edge of the door mounts is not as deep as the door is thick.

The cockpit detailing looks like it was copied from the Accurate Miniatures kits to a large extent. The curved floor that is actually the top of the center wing section is correctly represented. There are separate parts for the side details, and there are reasonably good representations of the seat, control column, and instrument panel. To cover the finished cockpit, both standard and Malcolm hood canopies are provided, but they are only in the fully closed position. The aft windows are each separate pieces, but there is no edge on the fuselage onto which to glue them. This means that they only butt up to the curved fuselage areas where they are mounted. This makes gluing them into place a bit tedious, and it must be rather precise. It also means that the bond between the aft windows and the fuselage is not very strong.

Other clear parts are provided for most of the lights, although the small white light, located low on the trailing edge of the rudder, is missing. We added this with thin plastic rod and painted the lens white.

Pylons are provided for the underwing stores, and 75-gallon fuel tanks and 250-pound bombs are included as options to go on them. Both of these are correct for the P-51A, while the fuel tanks would be appropriate for the F-6A and Mustang Mk. IA.

The instructions are very poor. ICM uses a set of letters to identify colors that parts are to be painted, but the chart that identifies what colors those letters represent does not match up, nor does it include all of the colors. Assembly instructions are simply exploded views that lack any written directions or sequence of assembly.

The worst part of the kit is the decal sheet. We were concerned about its quality, so we first tried working with a decal that was for the markings option that we were not using. Sure enough, the decal disintegrated when it was immersed in water. We then gave the decals two good coats of clear decal film, and once it had dried completely, we cut out the decals carefully. While the decals held together with the added clear film, they did not stick to the model well, and they tended to curl up as they dried. Only after much patient use of setting solutions and some clear coating did we get them to adhere to the model. This still left some obvious decal film that had to be painted over. This is more of a problem than it would be with most other kits, because there are few if any after-market decals options for Allison-engined Mustangs.

With some work, the ICM kits can be used to build reasonably nice models of Mustangs. We were pleased with how our review sample turned out. But they are not as good as the Accurate Miniatures kits and their subsequent re-releases by Academy that are still easily available.

Halberd Models XP-51, Mustang Mk. I

Halberd Models is a Ukrainian manufacturer specializing in limited-run but high-quality cast resin conversion sets and full kits. Their subject matter is unique, covering unusual aircraft that mainstream manufacturers ignore. Their product line includes cast resin kits of the XP-51, Mustang Mk. I, and Mustang Mk. X in 1/48th scale. Variant-specific details differ between the three kits, but they also share many overlapping characteristics. Each kit has between forty-one and forty-three parts. The fuselage is conventional, split into left and right halves. The wings come as a single piece. Surfaces are as smooth as any mainstream plastic kit, and surface details are rather exquisite with finely engraved and accurate panel lines and rivet details. The fit of the parts is also excellent for a cast resin kit. While some seam cleanup is necessary for the upper and lower fuselage seams and the fuselage-to-wing joints, no excessive work is required. In fact, a few builders have commented that these are among the best cast resin kits they have ever built.

A full cockpit is provided to include the gunsight, instrument panel, a correctly curved cockpit floor, sidewall details, the ear-

Halberd Models from Ukraine produces cast resin kits of the XP-51 and the Mustang Mk. I in 1/48th scale. They are essentially the Accurate Miniatures Allison-powered Mustangs but cast in resin with all-new, high-fidelity surface details. Co-author Haagen Klaus used the Halberd XP-51 kit to build the second of the two XP-51s as it appeared at Wright Field for flight tests, following its arrival there in December 1941. The canopy was opened with a razor saw and Eduard photoetched seat belts were added. The model was painted mostly with Alclad II paints along with AK Xtreme Metal and AK Super Chrome products applied to some sections of the airframe. (Klaus)

ly-style Schick-Johnson seat, the radios, the aircraft battery, and rollover bar. The dial faces for the instrument panel are provided as a decal. The main landing gear well is integrally molded into the bottom of the wing. It features a relatively good level of general detail (but see below). Thankfully, the main landing gear and tail wheel assembly are molded around a brass rod, so they will have no issues supporting the weight of the model. The main gear struts look great and only lack the brake lines. Landing gear well doors are likewise well detailed, and the kit includes the gear door actuators. The radiator exhaust door can be positioned opened or closed. The canopy and side windows are cast in clear resin and possess good visual quality, though one may wish to polish them even clearer. However, the windscreen and canopy are cast as a single piece, and a razor saw would be needed to separate them.

Variant-specific features are well represented, including the different propeller types, engine nacelle shapes and configurations (especially with the Merlin-powered Mustang Mk. X), radiator inlet configuration, a standard U. S. control stick, and a control column with an oval handle for RAF aircraft.

The Halberd family of Allison-powered early P-51s have many excellent points, but a few observations do come to mind. The cockpit is good, but the level of detail (especially the instrument panel) can certainly be enhanced by adapting detail parts for other early Mustangs or by scratchbuilding desired details. Shoulder harnesses and lap belts are not included, and their addition would enhance the cockpit even further. It is also quite clear that the wings and fuselage appear to be based off a copy of the Accurate Miniatures kit, right down to the specific details of the integrally molded landing gear well. All other issues aside, the gear wells have somewhat generalized details, but the inboard left and right gear well walls are conspicuously devoid of all detail.

Overall, these Halberd early P-51s do a fine job of representing the XP-51 and the Mustang Mk. I. Each is priced at $85.00. The quality, rare subject matter, and the labor behind hand-cast parts justifies the price tag, and it is also less expensive than many of today's mainstream kits. Anyone with some experience with cast resin kits will build Halberd's Mustangs with ease, and for anyone who has not built in this medium before, any one of these Mustangs would make an excellent introduction to the world of cast resin kits.

1/32nd SCALE KITS

Hobbycraft P-51-NA, P-51A, Mustang Mk. IA, and A-36A

As of early 2025, the only injection-molded kits of Allison-engined Mustangs that have been released in 1/32nd scale have been from Hobbycraft of Canada. The first of these was a P-51-NA that was issued in 2005, and that same year a P-51A was also issued. These were followed by an RAF Mustang Mk. IA in 2007 and an A-36A in 2009. While the basics of these four kits remained the same, each had different parts

Hobbycraft has released kits of the P-51-NA, P-51A, Mustang Mk. IA, and the A-36A in 1/32nd scale, but they are no longer in production and are very difficult to find. All of the kits were basically the Accurate Miniatures kits scaled up to 1/32nd scale, and all were essentially the same kit, but each had optional parts to build the specific variant that each kit represents. Chip Michie used the P-51A kit straight out of the box to build this model of the commander's aircraft from the 1st Air Commando Group. (Michie)

to build the specific variant that each kit represented. Unfortunately, these are no longer in production, and the most difficult part of building one will simply be finding it. Our searches online to find one proved unsuccessful. Fortunately, Chip Michie agreed to build the P-51A he had in his stash for our review.

To produce these kits, Hobbycraft received permission from Accurate Miniatures to scale up their 1/48th scale Allison-engined Mustangs (reviewed above) to 1/32nd scale. Accordingly, to a large extent these kits are simply bigger versions of the Accurate Miniatures kits, but there are some differences. The plastic in the Hobbycraft kits is soft, and the surface has a textured look. Some light sanding and the application of paint will reduce this to being unnoticeable. There is some flash present on several parts, but this is easily removed during preparation. The trailing edges of the wings and tail surfaces are too thick and should be sanded down. Surface detailing is recessed and reasonably well done. Like the Accurate Miniatures kits, the flaps are molded integral to the wings, so displaying them in the lowered position requires some plastic surgery and modification to the separated flaps.

Another issue shared with the Accurate Miniatures kits is that the main gear wells are molded as part of the lower wings, and this means that the walls are even with the openings for the wells. The rear wall, in particular, should be recessed aft into the wing structure, and this inaccuracy is rather noticeable in 1/32nd scale.

Clear parts provide the standard framed canopy with all parts molded together to have the canopy added in the closed position. Optional parts provide the choice of displaying the canopy open to better reveal the cockpit detailing. The windscreen and the canopy are a bit undersized. The instrument panel and details on the sides and floor of the cockpit are adequate, but they can easily be enhanced with a little detailing. The floor is the correct curved design that is simply the top of the center wing structure. There are two different seats provided, but neither has any seat belts nor the shoulder harness. These certainly should be added in 1/32nd scale. The gunsight is rather poor, and some modelers will want to replace it or build a better one from scratch.

Standard and weighted tires are provided with a faint diamond tread. These are best replaced with aftermarket resin wheels and tires. The hubs are separate parts, and this makes painting much easier.

The very front of the fuselage where it meets the spinner is misshaped, being a bit concave in shape, and this needs to be corrected with some putty and sanding. Some filling and sanding will be needed in several places, particularly where the wing assembly joins the fuselage and also around the intake for the radiator.

The P-51-NA and P-51A kits have the openings for the two cowl-mounted .50-caliber machine guns, so these have to be filled in and sanded smooth. They are fine for the A-36A and Mustang Mk. IA kits. The wing guns for the A-36A and P-51A are incorrect. The openings are a bit oversized, and they are in line with the dihedral of the wing. They should be parallel to the ground line, meaning that the outer gun in each wing should be lower than the inner gun. This inaccuracy is quite noticeable and needs to be corrected.

The instructions are very poor. There is no text, and the illustrations leave a lot to be desired. The painting information is on the back of the box, but it only consists of a listing of colors with no indication as to where the colors are used.

Like the Accurate Miniatures kits, the gaps in the dive brakes on the A-36A kit are open into the wing, and this results in a see-through effect. Adding some plastic card on the inside surface of each wing where the brakes are located will solve this issue. Likewise, the hole where the landing lights are mounted is open back into the wing, so adding some plastic card to fill in this area is recommended. This is particularly important for the A-36A with its large dual-light arrangement.

The Mustang Mk. IA kit provides a camera for the aft cockpit, and bombs and 75-gallon fuel tanks are included for the P-51A and A-36A kits. These are not as good as they should be, and we recommend using spare bombs or fuel tanks from other Mustang kits in 1/32nd scale as replacements. Fortunately, several of the other kits offer bomb and fuel tank options that leave spares of unused parts available, and these kits from Hobbycraft are a good place to use them.

While these kits are only average in quality and accuracy, they remain the only injection-molded 1/32nd scale kits of Allison-engined Mustangs that have ever been issued. As mentioned at the beginning of this review, they are no longer in production and are very difficult to find. Hopefully, they will be reissued in the future, or another company will produce better 1/32nd scale kits of these important Mustang variants.

FINAL THOUGHTS

The state of modeling in 2025 for Allison-powered early Mustangs is mixed. In various ways, these aircraft are somewhat neglected. Part of this is due to the "P-51D phenomenon." The scale modeling industry is certainly biased towards this legendary Mustang variant, and the market shows that there is a great deal of popularity surrounding the P-51D. Another element is mystique: the widespread misconception of early Mustangs as aircraft that did not live up to their potential, serving as underdeveloped interim versions until the P-51D perfected the design. Of course, this is a myth extensively debunked by this publication. For these, and whatever other reasons, Allison-powered early Mustangs have not received comparable attention.

There is clearly a requirement for 1/144th scale kits, and they need to be of contemporary quality. In 1/72nd scale, there are no real standouts or kits that reflect today's state-of-the-art. The best in that scale could be considered a tie between Academy and Brengun kits, but the Italeri kit is also a reasonable option. Sadly, none can be considered as excellent kits. In 1/48th scale, the thirty-year-old Accurate Miniatures kits (since reissued under the Academy label) remain the best options, but the ICM kit is also worth considering. The Halberd Models kits are more esoteric in nature and will appeal to the modeler who wants to build something a little different from the production variants. The Hobbycraft P-51-NA, P-51A, Mustang Mk. IA and A-36 represent every offering of Allison-engined variants in 1/32nd scale, but there is a lot of distance between them and the Tamiya P-51D in terms of quality and detail. Further, they are out of production and it is very difficult to find one. Careful attention to detail and use of aftermarket enhancements can lead to very good, if not excellent, Allison-powered early P-51 models built from several of the kits reviewed here.

Still, the lineage of Allison-engined aircraft awaits the attention they rightly deserve in the form of newly tooled high-quality kits. With Eduard's progressive release of 1/48th and 1/72nd scale P-51Ds followed by P-51B/Cs, we hope the rumor is true that Eduard intends to produce kits of the *entire* Mustang lineage, and that these early P-51 variants are next on their list.

The Detail & Scale Series

Get the digital edition!

The digital edition offers the same great content, with every high-resolution photograph expandable to full screen on your computer or mobile device. All at a much lower price. Visit our website at

www.detailandscale.com

to learn about all of our digital and print publications.

www.detailandscale.com

ABOUT THE AUTHORS

Author Bert Kinzey graduated from Virginia Tech in 1968 with a degree in Business Administration. Upon graduation, he was commissioned a second lieutenant in the U. S. Army and was sent to the Army's Air Defense School at Fort Bliss, Texas. During his eight years as an officer, Bert commanded a Hawk guided missile battery just south of the DMZ in Korea. Later he originated, wrote, and taught classes on the air threat, military air power, and air defense suppression at Fort Bliss.

In 1976, Bert resigned from active duty, but his reputation for being knowledgeable about all aspects of military air power soon led to his taking a civilian position as a subject matter expert on the air threat and world airpower with the Department of Defense. Bert has also flown with active, Reserve, and National Guard squadrons on training missions to observe the conduct and procedures of air-to-air and air-to-ground combat. As both an officer and a civilian, Bert often briefed military and political leaders of the United States and other nations on subjects related to air power, the air threat, and air defense.

While he was working for the Department of Defense, Bert started Detail & Scale, a part-time business to produce a new series of books on military aircraft. The Detail & Scale Series of publications was the first to focus on the many details of military aircraft to include cockpits, weapon systems, radars and avionics systems, differences between variants, airframe design, and much more. These books became so successful that Bert resigned from his position with the Department of Defense and began writing and producing books full time. He also began a second series called Colors & Markings. Each book in this series focused on a specific aircraft type and illustrated the paint schemes and markings of every unit that had flown that aircraft. Bert has also produced several stand-alone books on military aviation subjects. In January 2002, Bert produced his one-hundredth aviation publication.

In June 2004, health issues caused Bert to retire from his work, and his two series of aviation books came to an end. But in 2011, the Detail & Scale website was created at www.detailandscale.com, and a Detail & Scale Facebook page was also begun. By the end of 2013, Bert had completed the first new title in the Detail & Scale Series in almost ten years, and more books followed. This new venture was made possible through a partnership with Rock Roszak.

Bert currently lives in Blacksburg, Virginia, with his wife Lynda. They have two children and five grandchildren.

Born and raised on the east end of Long Island, co-author Haagen Klaus grew up around airplanes. His love of aviation started early and was encouraged by his parents, his uncle (a USAF colonel), and a community of mentors at Grumman Aircraft Corporation's flight test center at Calverton, New York. In college, Haagen considered an ROTC route towards a career in military aviation, but he was unexpectedly drawn to a different path – archaeology. Haagen graduated with degrees in anthropology, archaeology, biological anthropology, and studio art from SUNY Plattsburgh (BA, 2000), Southern Illinois University (MA, 2003), and The Ohio State University (Ph.D., 2008).

Since 2002, he has directed a multi-national, multi-decade bioarchaeological research project in the deserts of Peru. Haagen is a widely published professor at George Mason University just outside Washington, D.C., training students in human anatomy, paleopathology, bone biology, South American archaeology, and forensic anthropology. His research and teaching have garnered numerous awards and he was named a National Geographic Explorer in 2014. Since 2003, Haagen has also served in consultancy roles to law enforcement, from local police departments to the Department of Homeland Security.

Haagen has been building aircraft models since he was seven years old. In 1997, he became an active member of the International Plastic Modeler's Society. Haagen has worked in hobby retail and was co-founder of IPMS/Champlain Valley with Frank Baehre (Lt.Col., USAF, ret.) and of the CAN-AM Con model contest series that continues today. He is currently the vice president of IPMS/Northern Virginia. His scale models have won awards at local, regional, and national-level competitions. Haagen also serves at the Smithsonian Institution's National Air and Space Museum to help preserve their scale aircraft model collection.

A Detail & Scale publication was the first aircraft reference book that Haagen ever saw when he was young. In 2014, Bert Kinzey began a conversation with him at the IPMS/USA Nationals that evolved into Haagen's roles as a contributing photographer and the editor of Scale Modeling News and Reviews. Haagen has since reviewed hundreds of kits, aftermarket detail sets, decals, and books for readers around the world on the website and on social media. He lives in Fairfax, Virginia. This is Haagen's fifth book with Detail & Scale.

Printed in Great Britain
by Amazon

58368647R00059